UP THE KASBAH

By the same editor
Out of the Shadows -
A History of the pioneering London gay groups & organisations, 1967-99

Gay expats go....

UP THE KASBAH

in the steps of Wilde, Gide and Genet.

1890–1990

With a Foreword by Peter Robins

Editor: Tony Walton

Historians: Paul Horler & Adrian Hammond

Technical editor: Clive Clareton

Bona Street Press

Up the Kasbah
Edited by Tony Walton

First published 2011 by Bona Street Press
BM Box 7128, London WC1N 3XX

ISBN **978-0-9566091-1-3**

Set in Garamond, Times New Roman and Nimrod MT

CONTENTS

Part Three: In the region of Tangier

Foreword
by Peter Robins

This delightful book is a pleasing evocation of three North African territories mainly in the early and middle years of the twentieth century. It will be of lasting value to social historians as well as to older gay readers, not many of them by any means from the financial background or having the social assurance of the numerous distinguished and often artistically gifted men mentioned in the book.

But is this all about exploitation by latter-day imperialists? Certainly not. By 1970 package holidays to the Mediterranean were very much in vogue for families, at reasonable prices. And for the bachelor (or the not-so-happily married) "Wonderful Copenhagen" or "Tulips from Amsterdam" were no longer just wistful choruses sung in discreet bars in side streets in our larger cities. At last, they could actually go to all the faraway places.

One further point is touched on by the book. Teenagers and young men around the Mediterranean were traditionally lively, easy-going and lustful, unlike our own more inhibited lads at the same period of time.

Should there be a sequel? Why not? It is up to you, dear reader. If this delightful survey prompts you to go and discover Tangier, Tunis and Algiers for yourself, then do it and then return to tell us how much human pleasures have changed since the days this book describes.

In the meantime, however, I hear rumours about memoirs of South Morocco being assembled (Agadir, el Jadida, Marrakech, etc.). I feel sure I will enjoy them as much as I did this collection.

PETER ROBINS has published five novels:
Easy Stages, Ruined Boys, Stony Glances, Survivors, Touching Harry.
Also four volumes of short stories:
The Gay Touch, Summer Shorts, Undo Your Raincoats and Laugh and *Our Hero Has Bad Breath.*
One volume of autobiography: *Visits, a pre-war childhood.*

He has worked as a book and theatre critic for The Times, Times Educational Supplement, the BBC and LBC.

He lives in Outer South London.

Acknowledgements

The editor would like to thank the many people who have contributed their memories of old Tangier, North Morocco, Algeria and Tunisia.

Each contributor has given us a unique and interesting account, but a very special word of thanks to six of them, in alphabetical order:-

First to David Aprahamian-Liddle for his help setting up the final interview (described in the epilogue) as well as for the information on Peter Wildeblood. Second to Adrian Hammnd for his work on Gide/Wilde, as well as his interviewing some of the characters, translating an interview from the French and giving us some of his own memories of Tunisia. Third to Paul Horler who has given us a huge amount of his historical research into Tangier as well as providing us with many postcards and photos from his wonderful private collection. Fourth to Alan Moriarty who has done most of the proof-reading, as well as writing several contributions himself, and producing the map. Fifth to Peter Robins for very kindly writing the Foreword, as well as giving his memories of two different countries. Sixth to Rowan Tudor who set up one of the interviews (with Peter Kendall) and who contributed many of his own memories of different places, as well as being one of the characters in the book himself!

Many thanks also to the other contributors:-
Crispin Arnold, Martin Croydon, Horace Gendell, Ray Harvey-Amer, Fritz Heiner, John Hoopard, Brendon Knight, Peter Lever, Peter Middlegate, Charles Naden, Vincent Norwich, Paul Okken, Sam Raynor, Jerome Santos and Jim Tate.

The Introduction mentions the fact that several of the contributors have now passed away and, although they are not in the list above, we are very grateful to them and we cherish their memories (in both senses).

A very big thank you lastly to Clive Clareton, without whose help on the technical side the project would not have been possible.

A bibliography has been included at the back and many of those books have been essential reading for many of our contributors, both for checking general information and for inspiration.

Every effort has been made to locate the copyright owners of photos used but some of them go back a very long way and this has often been difficult. In the event that anyone sees a photo for which they have the copyright they should contact the publishers.

Editor's Introduction

Having compiled and edited this collection of various memories, memoirs and opinions, I am extremely happy to commend them to you. It provides an interesting and hitherto mainly unwritten picture of life amongst the gay expats of North Morocco, Algeria and Tunisia, chiefly in the first 75 years of the Twentieth Century.

How did this project come about? It started off in 2002 by recording conversations/interviews with gays who had visited these areas (especially Tangier) in former days, and these form an important part of the book. All of them are interesting but the one with the author Patrick Thursfield, recorded in our Epilogue, was especially significant.

In one sense it's a pity it has taken eight years to put it all together, but in another sense it has been good – since during all that time one person has put me in touch with someone else, and then that second person knew other people who went to North Africa in the old days, and so on. So the list of contributors has become unexpectedly very long and impressive.

Apart from people's written contributions, we are in fact including eight interviews with people who knew parts of Morocco in the old days, in the 50s and 60s. These interviews all took place in the first years of this century, yet very sadly and surprisingly, <u>four out of eight</u> of the gentlemen interviewed on Morocco, including Patrick Thursfield, have now passed away. In addition, two of those who gave us stories for the Tunisia section have also died. We think we owe it to all of them to include their tales, as they contain a record which would otherwise be forgotten.

I have tried to put all these interviews, plus all the written contributions, together in the most logical order and, where two separate accounts have been written about the same person or place, to amalgamate them into one account. This has not always been easy but I hope readers will follow the sequence and enjoy reading all the contributions.

Inevitably, when a book has several authors, the type of material and the style changes and varies. I feel this is one of its strengths, however, since it greatly adds variety – sometimes the readers being offered serious or thoughtful material but elsewhere light-hearted or gossipy contributions.

Why the title "Up the Kasbah"?

Well, as you know the Kasbah was the highest part of most of the old cities in North Africa, so we can imagine ourselves looking down at those gay expats and holiday-makers in the lower part of the town and seeing what they are getting up to down there. (In Chapter 2 we hear about Oscar Wilde actually leading André Gide up into the Kasbah of Algiers and them having an interesting evening together up there!)

The title of course has a humorous, double-entendre side to it, and we have often found ourselves hearing and retelling amusing anecdotes about the life of the gay expats in the cities – their adventures and their antics.

View from the Tangier Kasbah, c. 1940

But there is a serious side to the book as well. It seeks to record an important part of gay history – where gay men and women have gone abroad often to find the kind of freedom they were not always able to find in their own country. As it says in another chapter, when one writes that Tangier used to be "gay friendly" it's well worth remembering that it was so at a time (the 1920s through to the 1960s) when the rest of the world was mostly anything but.

Why the sub-title:
"In the steps of Wilde, Gide & Genet"?

By this we mean that nearly all the places mentioned in this book were visited by one or another of those three distinguished writers in the past. We are taking you round some of those North African places they went to, as well as some others nearby, and describing how gays used to go to those same holiday destinations throughout the greater part of the twentieth century. Some of those gay visitors settled in those cities and become expats too, often as they found the environment better than the one back home.

Least of all have they gone to Algeria, since sadly that country went through turmoil in the 20th century and there was little tourism left of any kind. On the other hand our earliest chapters chronologically *are* about Algeria since it was once the "in place" to go, with famous visitors including Wilde, Douglas and Gide. We have also been pleased to find two gentlemen who went there only about forty years ago – few others did so.

We are including stories of the other North African holiday destinations too, such as Hammamet and Sousse in Tunisia, visited by Gide as early as 1893. We are likewise mentioning Asilah, Larache and Fez, all within fairly easy reach of Tangier and often visited for short or long spells by those staying there, and with the French gay author Genet making Larache his final home.

But most of all did they go to the city of Tangier. So Tangier, in Part Two, will be our biggest section. The story of life in that city has been made known through several books. We do not want to compete with those books but we do want to concentrate on the memories of the mainly *gay* expats, including a lot of material only recently come to light, plus some very interesting compilations by our resident historian, Paul Horler.

We hope you will enjoy reading the book as much as we have enjoyed putting it together.

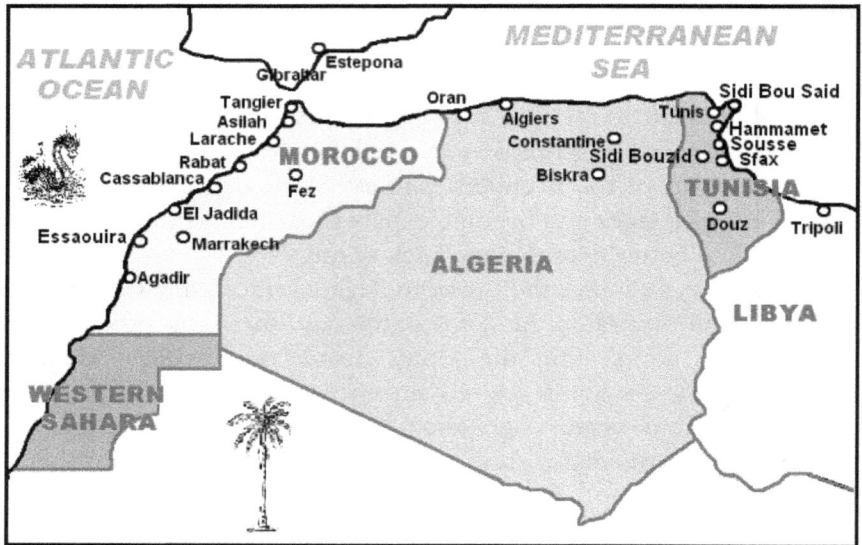

Sketch-map showing the main locations mentioned in the text

PART ONE:

ALGERIA AND TUNISIA

1
Old Algiers, gay capital of world?
by Tony Walton

Old Algiers

So much, rightly, has been written about gay events and people in Tangier that we can so easily forget the pre-eminence of Algiers for gay people, at least up until World War One.

The Encyclopaedia of Homosexuality states that "Algiers was the most Turkish city in North Africa, in fact the most Turkish city outside of Turkey. During the sixteenth and seventeenth centuries, it was possibly *the leading homosexual city in the world.*" (our italics).

In the late nineteenth century and early twentieth, the cities of Algiers and Tunis were to become almost the favourite places for gay gentlemen to visit. It seems as if that corner of North Africa had become the main meeting place of the gay intelligentsia, a role which Tangier took over later between the wars. For example the gay writers Henri de Montherlant, André Gide (of whom much more in the next chapter) and Ronald Firbank all visited the Tunis/Algiers area. And each of these writers dealt with gay culture fairly openly in their writing.

One could very easily read the last sentence without seeing the huge historical significance. The fact is that writers of the late nineteenth century were, as a group, the very first in Western Europe to express their homosexuality openly in their work. There were few writers like them in the eighteenth century nor in the early nineteenth, except perhaps for Byron. They could be called the first "school" of gay writers outside of Greece and Rome. (England had its own writers like Carpenter, Havelock Ellis, Housman and Hopkins who were around the same time also expressing similar sentiment.) For writers to express their gay feeling in their work, and to each other through discussion, was hitherto almost unknown.

The sad and ironic thing was that, just as they were developing this sense of identity, the law in Britain was suddenly and unexpectedly changed, with the Labouchere amendment of 1885, very much for the worse.

So perhaps the feeling of being out of sympathy with the society in which they lived may have encouraged them to try new places with a different culture, such as Southern Italy, Tunis, Algiers and later Tangier. Maybe it was these relaxing Mediterranean visits, and meeting each other whilst there, which helped them in their development as artists and in the expression of their sexuality.

The three best known literary visitors to what we now call Algeria and Tunisia were André Gide, Oscar Wilde and Lord Alfred Douglas, so Adrian Hammond will devote the whole of the next chapter to summarising all their adventures there.

2
Wilde & Gide in North Africa
by Adrian Hammond

When you hear about the travels of these famous men in North Africa you are slightly bewildered by the frequency and speed of their movements, so it's worth telling you how they would have travelled in those days.

Travel between Paris and Marseilles was quite easy by train, and from there they would go by boat to either Tunis or Algiers, which were about equidistant from Marseilles. Algeria and Tunisia were both part of French North Africa, and the French had built a railway between the two ports of Algiers and Tunis which went inland to "cut off the corner" of North Tunisia. Now this railway was the key to several events in the story, because it had a branch which passed near the two very agreeable inland towns of Blidah and Biskra. Many of the events in this chapter are centred on those two towns, especially the beautiful oasis town of Biskra, built on a river.

Another easy transport route for them was by boat from Tunis to Sousse across the Bay of Hammamet, and these boats would call in halfway across at the little port of Hammamet itself. So you can see how Sousse and Hammamet came into the story.

André's first trip

André Gide had had a repressed childhood in late nineteenth century France and he found release from this through travelling and then writing about those travels. After his first trips to North Africa in the 1890s (he spent time in Algiers, Tunis, Sousse and Hammamet), he rebelled against his early background and "gave expression to a pagan value system that was for him a self-liberation from the morals and conventions of his upbringing." (Encyc. of Homosexuality).

But let's start with his earliest travels. In 1893 the young André, a poet and living in Paris, decided to explore North Africa with his artist friend Paul Laurent. Paul felt the scenes he would see there would be wonderful to paint, and for André it was an exercise in escaping from the restrictions of his life and to "find himself". (Both of them came from rich families and neither of them seems to have had any small thing to worry about like earning money –

development as artists was all that mattered to either; in André 's case Mama was always available to help when needed).

Sailing to Tunis the pair enjoyed a tour of the town by a native young guide named Cecy, the first of several guides/ companions. Then travelling by horse and carriage they paid a visit to the inland holy city of Kairouan, from which they continued to Sousse on the coast. From Sousse they planned to go further south.

Encounter in Sousse

However, Gide was beginning to go down with signs of lung illness and as his father had only just died of tuberculosis he was naturally very anxious. So they decided to stay longer than expected in Sousse to allow him to rest.

One day whilst staying there, Paul accompanied André into an area outside the Medina on the outskirts of the city where he was doing paintings of some locals. His guide Ali, however, suggested that while Paul was busy painting, André should follow him into the sand-dunes. Here we'll let André tell his own story: [1]:

"I had already noticed (the young guide) on the previous day among the troop who loitered in the neighbourhood of the hotel. He wore a chechia on his head like the others and nothing but a coat of coarse linen and baggy Tunisian trousers... He seemed more reserved or more timid than his companions, so that as a rule they were beforehand with him; but that day, I don't know how it was, I went out without any of them seeing me, and all of a sudden it was he who joined me at the corner.

"The hotel was situated in a sandy district on the outskirts of Sousse... Ali led me up among the sandhills... we soon reached a kind of funnel or crater, the rim of which was just high enough to see the surrounding country and give a view of anyone coming.

"As soon as we got there, Ali flung the coat and rug down on the sloping sand; he flung himself down too, and stretched on his back, with his arms spread out on each side of him, he looked at me

---

[1] Taken from his book 'If It Die', although most of this section, as well as the section quoted further on (pages 13-14), is omitted from the Penguin English version of the 1950s, since it was considered too 'explicit' .

and laughed. I was not such a simpleton as to misunderstand his invitation; but I did not answer it at once and I sat down myself.

I was extremely curious as to what would happen next. I waited! I wonder today at my fortitude... And I watched his laughter slowly fade away, and an expression of sadness cloud his charming face.

'Good-bye, then,' he said.

"But I seized the hand he held out to me and tumbled him on to the ground. In a moment he was laughing again. The complicated knots of the strings that served him for girdle did not long trouble his impatience. The garment fell, and flinging away his coat, he emerged naked as a god. Then he raised his slight arms for a moment to the sky and dropped laughing against me. Though his body was burning, it felt as cool and refreshing to my hands as shade.

"How beautiful the sand was! In the lovely splendour of that evening light, what radiance clothed my joy!"

André, however, decided to say nothing to anyone about the incident, not even to Paul. In any case, the two decided to return to Tunis where André could receive some medical help. They took the boat from Sousse and called in for a fairly long stay en route in Hammamet (purely for health reasons, of course!).

Hammamet house where Gide stayed, with Charm Beach in distance

A visit to Biskra

One reason why André had kept his gay experience completely secret for a while from his friends was that he still wanted to marry his cousin Madeleine.

So one might have thought that after all their adventures André and Paul would now think about returning home – perhaps to see Madeleine again or maybe (perish the thought) to do some work. Yet, after Hammamet, they couldn't resist travelling further to the paradise oasis town of Biskra, in what we now call Algeria.

Biskra, c.1895, described as Algeria's Eden

Paul was understandably worried about André´s health, however, so they employed the services of a young black named Athman to look after them. André described Athman thus: "He was the best and most honest boy in the world, incapable of taking advantage of anyone and with as little ability to make money as a poet – always ready on the contrary to spend and give away all he had." The youth was completely devoted to them, carrying Paul's easel with him, for instance, when he went out on painting sprees, or making sure André befriended only the best kind of locals.

André was to remain friends with Athman for years, and indeed would have taken him back to Paris had not Mama and Madeleine stopped him from doing so. Luckily a friend named Henri Gheon agreed to bring the young man to Paris, so the friendship lasted a long time.

Back to our immediate story. Once settled in Biskra, in order to prove his manhood and get himself ready for marriage, André now embarked on a heterosexual relationship, a rather odd kind of threesome with himself, Paul and the lovely young servant girl Meriem – plus of course the devoted Athman looking on and attending to all their eating, drinking (and possibly other) needs.

However, into this slightly strange paradise suddenly arrived a fifth character, and we wonder if readers can guess who it was?

Yes, it was Mama. Undeterred by travelling all the way from Paris to Biskra via Marseilles and Tunis, she was determined to see how her son André was getting on and whether he was behaving himself. (André in his letters home had probably been too honest about his locations and activities).

André was glad to see her in one sense, as he was getting short of funds. But she was not at all pleased about his domestic arrangements and was worried about his health. So after a few weeks of this maternal supervision she persuaded him to (eventually) come home to Europe and take a health cure in Switzerland.

She herself, perhaps to everyone's relief, then returned with her maid to Paris.

Oscar and Bosie's first travels

On André's way to his health-cure in Switzerland he met his old friends Oscar Wilde and Lord Alfred Douglas in Florence and told them about the joys of Tunis and Biskra, although assuring them that his interest in the youths was purely platonic, of course. He hardly needed to tell them about the scene there, since by now the area of Algiers was becoming the fashionable place to visit for the trendy literati and the gay social elite.

Leaving André to take his health cure, Oscar and Bosie set off to explore for themselves, first to Algiers, where they got to know the scene with the local lads, and then the town of Blidah which was described in guide books as the "desert rose".

An early photo of Oscar

They stayed at the fashionable Hotel d`Orient in Blidah, from which Oscar wrote home to his friend Robbie:

"There is a great deal of beauty here...Bosie and I have taken to hashish: it is quite exquisite: three puffs of smoke and then all is peace and love. Bosie wakes up in the night and cries like a child for the best hashish...

"We have been on an excursion into the mountains of Kabylia – full of villages peopled by fauns. Several shepherds fluted on reeds for us. We were followed by lovely brown things from forest to forest. The beggars here have profiles, so the problem of poverty is easily solved."

Lord Alfred Douglas (Bosie)

André and Bosie

A few months after this, André had finished his health cure and was feeling much better. Yet, very understandably with December approaching, he considered he would feel even better if he left Switzerland and headed for North Africa again. (On a less cheerful note one must report that the whole Oscar Wilde and Lord Queensbury scandal had started to break in London; André had heard the bad news but had lost touch).

After a rough crossing to Algiers and then finding the weather in Blidah dismal and depressing, André decided to make for his beloved Biskra again. On arrival at his favourite hotel there, he looked up at the blackboard to view the names of current guests and was perturbed to see the names "Oscar Wilde and Lord Alfred Douglas" written up. His first reaction was to go quickly on to somewhere else, not wanting to get involved in the scandal.

However, he changed his mind and eventually met them.

Bosie was in fact especially pleased to see André as he wanted an excuse to leave Oscar and go and chase his latest love back in Blidah. On his own with André he told him frankly: "I hope you´re like me. I have a horror of women and only like boys."

André, who was trying to convince himself he was straight and bracing himself to marry Madeleine, was too shocked to reply. Not only shocked at the words themselves but also in realising that Bosie was perhaps using Oscar.

(One cannot help wondering if the modern gay view of Oscar and Bosie is clothed in political correctness – seeing them as gay lovers, yes, but ignoring the fact they spent a lot of their time together chasing younger males.)

Over dinner the three decided they would all go on to Algiers by train, as poor Oscar had to return to London for his trial..

On their arrival in Algiers a final quarrel broke out between Oscar and Bosie. Everyone else, including André, had been advising Oscar *not* to return to London as they felt it would end in disaster, but Bosie insisted that he did so.

The row ended with Bosie flouncing out and going off to Blidah to meet his new young paramour, leaving Oscar to face the music in London alone.

Up the Kasbah with Oscar

Before they left Algiers, however, Oscar took André right up into the Kasbah, the highest part of the town – to reach which they had to leave their carriage and make their way on foot up the steep little alleys. Again we will let André tell the story in his own words, from "If It Die":

"At first I did not understand what it was about the café (in the Kasbah) which attracted Wilde...I was dozing off in the strange topor of the place when a marvellous youth appeared at the half-opened door...He remained there quite a while, outlined against the blackness of the night. He seemed unsure if he should come in or not and I was worried that he would leave, but then he smiled when Wilde beckoned to him...

"He came and sat down opposite us on a little stool...He pulled a reed flute from his waistcoat and began to play exquisitely...

The Kasbah in old Algiers

"…Wilde told me that his name was Mohamed and that he (had been) Bosie´s boy. The reason why Mohamed had hesitated before coming in was because he could not see Lord Alfred. His large black eyes had that languorous look give by hashish, he had an olive complexion and I admired the way his fingers held the flute, the slimness of his boyish figure...

"We stayed like that without stirring for what seemed an eternity and I would have stayed there even longer had not Wilde all of a sudden broken the spell: 'Come,' he said."

(As they walk away Oscar asks André if he would like to "have" the young musician. André, after much hesitation and emotion, replies in a choking voice ´Yes!´).

"I had in my imagination overcome all my scruples. To be truthful I did not realise this myself. It was only when I replied 'Yes!' to him that I suddenly became aware of it."

Oscar roared with laughter, since his suspicions about André's gayness were now at last confirmed. He took André and Mohamed to a "short-stay" hotel where the relationship was consummated and André received satisfaction (he assures us in his writing) five times during the night

André wrote to Mama about other aspects of the trip:

"Algiers is marvellous and to think that I was going to leave the country without seeing it. Its streets are enchanted, the shadows there are even more mysterious than in the souks or under leafy trees...

"And Wilde! Wilde!! What more tragic life is there than his. If only he were more careful – But as he says himself 'I have put my genius into my life and I have only put my talent into my works. I know it, and that is the great tragedy of my life.' "

The next day, with André still trying to persuade him to stay in the paradise of Algiers, Oscar set off on his ill-fated and tragic trip back to London. For him there was little ahead except pain, ignominy and an early death.

Honeymoon in Algiers

Eventually young André returned to Paris.

The last thing one would then expect him to do was to get married, but that is exactly what he did. (He did tell his doctor about his homosexual tendencies and the doctor explained to him that these would all pass as soon as he was married. How helpful). And the last place you would think it wise for him to choose for his honeymoon would be Biskra, but that is where he chose. Mind you, the honeymoon lasted eight months – well, they needed a break after all that hard work, didn't they? – covering much of Italy too.

There is a passage in his book "If it Die" on the Algiers part of his honeymoon, which proves that the doctor was wrong in his predictions about Gide's gayness disappearing after marriage. The passage would be slightly funny were it not for the sad figure of his bride sitting with him and watching:

"A demon inhabited me. It never possessed me more imperiously than on our return from Biskra to Algiers. The Easter holidays had ended. In the train taking us from Biskra, three students returning to their lycée (schools for the over-fourteens) occupied the compartment next to ours. They were but half clothed, for the heat was tantalizing, and, alone in their compartment, were raising the roof, laughing and jostling. At each of the frequent stops the train made, by leaning out of the little window, my hand just reached the arm of a boy who amused himself by leaning toward me from the next window, laughingly entering into the spirit of the game; and I tasted excruciating delights in the touch of downy amber flesh...

"I would sit down, breathless and panting, and pretend to be absorbed by my reading. Madeleine, seated opposite me, said nothing, pretended not to see me, not to know me.

"On our arrival in Algiers, the two of us alone in the omnibus taking us to the hotel, she finally said to me in a tone more of sorrow than censure: 'You looked like either a criminal or a madman.' "

André Gide as a young man

Roses all the way

Still, the future for André was basically roses all the way, since he became more and more feted as a great author.

I believe Paul Horler is going to write about Angus Stewart, who lived in Tangier and who wrote the novel "Sandel" on the subject of an older/younger relationship. It seems strange to us in 2011 that such a book should have been a best-seller in the late 1960s, bearing in mind the current attitudes towards such things. Just the same could be said about André Gide, who also wrote on that theme yet who received nothing but praise in his lifetime, being awarded the Nobel Prize for literature in 1947, the first openly gay man to do so. So were the middle to late years of the twentieth century more tolerant in certain respects than our own age?

For André, occasional trips to Algeria and other destinations (he spent World War II in Tunis again) went on for several decades. He lived a happy and fulfilled life, full of plaudits, incredibly for fifty years after the death of his dear friend Oscar Wilde.

André Gide, circa 1948

3

Gay writers in Algeria & Tunisia

by Tony Walton

Algeria disappeared off the tourist map because of all the troubles and wars there, and Tangier had already replaced it as a gay destination during the years of the International Zone, c. 1925 to 1957. Luckily both Morocco and Tunisia obtained their independence reasonably peacefully, never having the same bitterness towards European people which sadly became prevalent in Algeria.

So one could say that Tangier arrived on the gay tourist scene later than the others, whilst Algiers' heyday came to an end sooner. Thus the third area of interest, Tunis and the Gulf of Hammamet, continued to play a quiet but consistent role in gay tourism for longer than both Algiers and Tangier.

We should mention that in medieval times the whole region of North West Africa, not too far from the Mediterranean, was known as the Maghreb, with the principal city sometimes at Fez in northern Morocco and sometimes at Kairouan in western Tunisia. So there has often been a connection between those two countries.

In addition, in more modern times Morocco and Tunisia have shared a similar history – with both of them under fairly benign and enlightened French control, and both achieving independence almost peacefully in the 1950s. Both have enjoyed several decades of stable government, so the ambience has become similar. Both are ex-French North African territories where French is the second official language, and both have expanded their tourist industries.

Many gays seem to have visited Algeria and Tunisia in the first half of the twentieth century. (It's even very possible that soldiers in North Africa during World War Two may have had some stories of friendship to tell, since the local populations often saw themselves as being liberated by the allied armies: for example, Robin Maugham, author of "The Wrong People", was in the Eighth Army from el Alamein right across to Tunisia, so his love for North Africans may well have started then.)

Both Tunisia and Algeria were French controlled but there was one important difference between the two territories, namely that Algeria was a colony and a part of the French Republic with many French settlers, whereas Tunisia was just an overseas territory and a protectorate. This meant that in the latter there was less tension between the two races.

Several gay authors visited both countries between the wars, for example Henri de Montherlant, who visited Algiers – where he met André Gide more than once. (Henri was, however, less than impressed with André, whom he said was drawing attention to himself in his flapping cloak and floppy pastoral hat – he considered both André's dress and his writing were pretentious.)

Sidi Bou Saïd (in North Tunisia)

Another important North African location in the fifty year period from 1918 to 1968 was Sidi Bou Saïd (sometimes spelt Sidi Bouzid), not far from Tunis and near the ruins of the ancient city of Carthage. This was, and is, a delightful small town/village on a wide headland, with its houses all painted in white and blue.

Sidi Bou Saïd is situated pleasantly on a headland

Just looking at the photos one can understand Sidi Bouzid being popular with tourists. But it was also situated close to Tunis, so it was an easy place for expats in Tunis to visit for a half-day out by train. In rather the same way, the expats of Tangier used to relax in Asilah when they needed a change from their big city, those of Sousse would take the metro to Monastir for a break, those of Agadir would visit the village of Taghazout for relaxation, or those of el Jadida would take a bus-ride out to their own seaside village of Sidi Bouzid. (The coincidence of the name Sidi Bouzid is that the two villages were probably named after the same Muslim saint).

Modern tourists to Tunisia usually fit in a trip to Sidi Bouzid

So this partly explains why it was so popular, but there was another aspect too. For some reason difficult to explain, and over a long period of time, Sidi Bou Saïd in North Tunisia became a place for the intellectuals and literati to visit and meet, almost like the Hampstead or Bloomsbury sets in London.

It was a favourite place firstly for André Gide, who sometimes went there when he was staying in Tunis. Secondly there was Henri de Montherlant (1895-1972) who lived in the south of France and was able to visit both Tunis and Sidi Bou Saïd regularly, although in later years his interest switched to Tangier. His main gay-themed works were a novel "The Boys" and a play "The City Whose Prince is a Child" (a quote from Bible). His novel"The Bachelors" is considered one of the greatest of the twentieth century.

Thirdly, Ronald Firbank (1886-1926) also called in at Sidi Bou Saïd, in fact spending most of his life travelling and writing his novels on the backs of large postcards. He stayed mostly in Tunis at the Tunisia Palace Hotel, but he much enjoyed trips by train to the famous village. His best-known book was a comic novel, "On the Eccentricities of Cardinal Pirelli", not published until after his death, perhaps because of its outrageous theme – with the cardinal seeking "special friendships" with choirboys but never quite succeeding. Firbank afterwards appears to have taken a liking to Sfax (2) even more, calling it "the most beautiful city in the world".

Later Sidi Bou Saïd became a favourite place of liberal-minded thinkers and writers, such as Simone de Beauvoir (1908-86), the partner of Jean Paul Sartre, and Sacheverell Sitwell (1897-1988), poet, art historian and biographer. Another very important visitor there also was the sexual philosopher Michel Foucault (1926-84).

Michel Foucault, the philosopher of gayness

---

2 There is a photo of Sfax on page 65

Michel Foucault, a Frenchman, was gay himself and was also the philosopher of gayness, remembered as the propagist of the new theory of "Social Construction". This proposed that words used by doctors, judges and teachers to describe human behaviour (e.g. "homosexuality") are used as weapons in the conflict between desire and power.

All of these thinkers must have appreciated the ambience of Sidi Bou Saïd, perhaps meeting each other and sharing ideas. They may not all have been gay themselves but each had an enlightened attitude towards gay people and had radical opinions, often opposed to the societies from which they came.

However, it was probably the massive expansion of straight tourism in the late 1960s and early 1970s which finished it off as a select village for intellectuals. A big city like Tangier could cope with different groups, but Sidi Bou Saïd was only small, so that once it became crowded-out with package holiday tourists and a favourite place for everyone to head towards, the elite and tranquil atmosphere inevitably vanished.

Interestingly, however, yet another Sidi Bouzid has achieved fame in very recent history, because the revolt against President Ben Ali of Tunisia started there in 2010. (The third Sidi Bouzid is in the south of Tunisia not too far from Sfax.)

A fruit-seller, Mohamed Bouazizi, becoming angry at police for confiscating his fruit stall (his only means of livelihood) when he was unable to pay the bribes they demanded, set fire to himself. Word spread about it throughout the country by means of mobile phones and the internet. The massive but peaceful protests lasting four weeks ended with the toppling of President Ben Ali, who took voluntary exile. At the time of writing, it appears to be spreading a wave of revolution throughout virtually the entire Arab world.

So perhaps the name "Sidi Bouzid" has some spiritual significance for freedom lovers even today.

4
Young gays visit Algeria
by Peter Lever and Peter Robins

Because the two Peters' accounts are all that we have on the Algerian scene in the later twentieth century, they are both specially welcome.

My trip to Algeria 1967 by Peter Lever

I was aged thirty and was teaching. Having saved up the amazing amount (for those days) of £500 I decided to take a year off teaching to visit Spain and North Africa, an area which has always fascinated me in my imagination. The other teachers thought I was mad, but I had no regrets about doing it, either then or now.

I started off with some friends, driving down through France, and they dropped me off at the Spanish border. From there I took the train and hitched my way down to Cadiz, from which I took the ferry across to Tangier.

Tangier was *wild* in those days, hopping with boys and young males of all ages. I quickly formed a friendship with an 18 year old, Azize, who I suppose was a rent boy but was surprisingly un-demanding, appreciating gifts but not asking for much money. He especially liked me buying him meals and a few items of clothing. I think I met him in the hammam (baths) and from there we went to one of the Medina hotels where you could have a room for 2 hours.

He certainly wasn't the jealous type and in fact he introduced me to friend number two, Jamil, who was desperate for friendship with a westerner but too shy and timid to put himself forward. He was very inexperienced and almost the opposite of the pushy type for which Tangier was famous.

When the time came for me finally (at the very end of this story) to leave North Africa and go back to Spain, Jamil saw me off on the ferry from Tangier to Algeciras. He went on and on waving, and I could see he was gently crying.

Before that sad farewell, however, I want to tell you about my trip into Algeria, because however lovely they were in Tangier I really did want to visit other places too.

I hitched my way from Tangier towards the Algerian border, mostly getting lifts in oil lorries. I have to say that wherever I went I met hardly anything except kindness, welcoming and friendliness. At night I would stay in little hostel places and there would sometimes be a bit of fun and games at night. More than once during the nights I could feel a hand coming towards me and my first reaction was that they were after my money – until I realised it was another bit of me that interested them.

There was one young guy who absolutely insisted that I played the active role – very unusual for an Arab. "You do jigga-jigga" he whispered to me, offering his rear – but he made it clear I was on no account to tell anyone else he had let me do it that way!

Another time, I was squeezed into the back of a 'deux-chevaux' between two Algerians. One of them cuddled me while the other started to explore me a bit more intimately. I felt that resistance would be useless.

Finally we got to the border with Algeria, but I had no visa. I was staying with two guys and they got the local police chief to come round and sort out my visa. He was a big man, who reeked of whisky and demanded they give him a meal (which he had smelt being cooked, though they were trying to hide it from him). He said that he would only see to my visa if I agreed to come back for the night with him. But the smell of whisky and his arrogance made me nervous.

I refused to go with him and went instead to the manse of the priest in charge of the local church. He was very nice, gave me some cheese and drink and let me sleep in the attic of his house – he said that he often had to offer this kind of hospitality. Well, I finally did manage to get the visa, with help in the end from the big guy, and I walked boldly across the frontier into Algeria. I then hitched lifts until I got to a big Algerian city called Constantine.

I found Constantine a beautiful and relaxing place with very open and friendly people who always wanted to help. It had a lovely square with old houses on three sides but the fourth side open, looking onto the mountains. The whole atmosphere was very French, with World War memorials, little boulevards, outdoor cafés.

The only problem was that I was now getting short of money – in those days you got it through telex and waiting for it to arrive at a given bank, which didn't always happen when it was supposed to.

They had of course only finished their war with the French about two years before, and my recollection is that the army was more or less in control, although everything seemed to be quite relaxed, not like a dictatorship.

Constantine in Algeria

They were surprisingly friendly to strangers and didn't seem to bear any grudges to Europeans after all the turmoil of the Algerian War, which had gone on for so many years. There was absolutely no sign of any fundamentalism and women dressed in a normal way.

As for the Algerian males, as in Morocco, I felt instinctively they would have approached fun and games with Europeans in a very light-hearted way, enjoying the occasional physical contact. (They were of course not allowed near their own women, so going with men was a pleasant and relaxing pastime, so long as they could play the masculine role.) I say "felt instinctively" as I really had no time to find out in a practical sense.

By this time I felt an urgent need to leave Algeria, firstly to sort out my money and secondly to see Azize and Jamil again back in Tangier. As I left Algeria, I remember thinking to myself that now all their troubles were over they could really open up their country successfully for tourism again, because it had been so popular, I believe, up until World War Two. And I also felt that gay men would be very well received there. I had no idea that things were going to get much worse rather than better, and I suppose the late 1960s/early 1970s (when I went) was just about the only time when things were fairly peaceful and settled, right up until about 2005.

My trip to Algeria 1971 by *Peter Robins*

In the early summer of 1971 I arrived at last in Oran in western Algeria. Twice I'd had to disappoint my friends who were teaching English as a foreign language there: first through my decision to venture no further than Tangier, then on a second occasion being part of a small media delegation there, busy being herded around to inspect everything – from new industrial developments based on oil, to the production of wine brewed from dates.

Finally I had made it, after a flight to Paris, a super-train south to Marseilles and then a comfortable ferry churning across the Mediterranean. As I stood on deck in the morning sunlight, admiring the clean white outline of Oran's buildings, I caught sight of my welcoming party, but it was an hour before I was free to join them. My feeling of wellbeing was rapidly deflated through being questioned for more than 50 minutes before allowed through Immigration. It seemed that the authorities found it difficult to accept that journalists actually do take holidays!

Once again in the sunlight I cheered up whilst being treated to a coffee and 'pain au chocolat' by the welcoming party. They were not surprised that my arrival had been treated with suspicion and warned me that I'd be followed, if wandering around as a solitary tourist. And so I was. Even at a university reception to which we were bidden, we made jokes that a mongrel dog mooching across the terrace was probably wired with a mini-microphone! None of this tempted me to think of migrating and becoming an expat.

My friends, all married or spoken for, could be of little help in that eternal quest of the bachelor – congenial, no-strings-attached company for a stay of short duration. So I set out, after a good night's rest, to look for myself. Where else to you suppose, dear reader, was there – other than the beach, the park but not, definitely not, the railway station. That, I felt, should be left to the desperate.

Oran in western Algeria

I chose the park and, fortunately that morning, so did Ahmed. He was taking his small sister for a walk. Just twenty-one, he was studying for a diploma in tourism, so we chatted away in Franglais, with plenty of laughs, until we parted for lunch.

But first we agreed to meet privately again in the afternoon, in the quieter surroundings of a local cinema. Ahmed, who was already in the foyer as I walked in, suggested the circle rather than the stalls. It was sparsely populated. What audience there was, consisted almost entirely of men of all ages and all of them in pairs. Though Ahmed and I saw the film four times in the course of the week, I doubt if he could have told you more of its content than I. The sound track provided background music, punctuated, from time to time, by cries from around the circle of "Vite, vite…j'arrive, j'arrive."

Whatever the local politics, human needs will find satisfaction.

5
Young gays visit Tunisia

We are grateful to Jim Tate, Ray Harvey-Amer and Vincent Norwich for digging into their memories and giving us these reminiscences of holidays in North Africa when they were young men.

A Sousse hotel dining room, to give a flavour of the 1970s

Winning a trip to Tunisia *by Jim Tate*

I had become very knowledgeable about the London gay scene in the 1970s, and I had also participated in many GLF activities. In 1976 when I was 28 I went on holiday to Tunisia with a gay person, Monas, whom I had met through GLF. He was a Sri Lankan, aged 38 and held a senior technical position at work. Because of my own technical background we became great friends, only mildly sexual.

Monas had entered a competition at his work and, along with twenty other work colleagues, had won a holiday for two in Sousse, Tunisia. Of course he didn't have a female partner, whereas all the other winners had heterosexual partners. This posed a problem for him as he hadn't as yet come out at work, but because of the influence that GLF had had on him, he decided to face the consequences by asking me to accompany him. This was particularly brave of him as he risked losing his job – he and I feared that (in those days) we might face hostility from others on the holiday.

I gladly accepted, as I have always enjoyed a challenge. But it was with trepidation that we arrived at the Sousse hotel at 10pm after being separated from the rest of our party during the flight. When the holiday representative introduced everybody, the other couples in the group were somewhat surprised to meet us, but they showed no hostility whatsoever. They soon all went to their rooms, but we went straight to the bar, where we quickly got to know the hotel staff!

The staff were all local men and were not in the least bit fazed by our overt display of gayness; some of them were clearly gay or bi themselves. In fact they told us that there were many guys cruising at night along the 1½ miles of beach from our beach hotel to the centre of Sousse. Most of the cruisers were locals with just a few holiday makers – they tended to be fairly young (although not kids) and were probably rent boys. It seemed natural to give them gifts, sometimes money, sometimes other things.

Monas and I were the last to arrive the next day for the early morning briefing with the holiday representative and about ten of the hotel staff, all of whom we had got to know very well the previous evening. The latter greeted us with great enthusiasm – much to the amazement of the other couples in our party, who thought that we must have stayed at the hotel before.

Monas and I soon became regulars at, I think, then the only gay bar in Sousse (probably Hotel Claridge). Both of us found local gay boyfriends. Mine was a very handsome 17 year old, who was I am afraid a bit of a rent boy, and due to his charm I nearly fell for his little tricks. He insisted on taking me to his uncle, in his forties, about three miles out of town, on the day before we were to return. Just as we arrived, my boyfriend suddenly disappeared. Then his "uncle" tried to rape me, but I managed to escape and get a passing taxi back to the hotel. This was the last I saw of that boyfriend!

During the Sousse holiday I hardly saw Monas as he was totally taken with his 21 year old boyfriend. On the last day Monas told me that he was madly in love and that he was not going to return to London; he would be staying on with his boyfriend as that was all that mattered to him. Since we were to board the coach to the airport at 4pm, I begged him to come back with us, but to no avail.

Everyone was on the coach at 4pm and ready to go, but I was hanging on to the coach door pleading with Monas, standing in the hotel entrance, to come with us. The coach driver was threatening to close the doors on me. Then just at the very last moment Monas saw sense and agreed to come, and I managed to get the coach driver to wait while someone got his bags. When we got back to Blighty, Monas took months to get over his romance. But he at least he kept his job.

Although from the description above it seems as though the local men (never women) were relatively out as gay, this was not the case. The cruising and meeting of gays was rather furtive and discreet. It would have been difficult to guess that the gay bar in Sousse was gay from a casual glance, as no Moroccan women went into bars anyway. Obviously the locals knew about it and tolerated it.

As far as I know, there was no hostility towards gays or towards the gay bar from the general public and the police. Although it was common to see young males holding hands and sometimes showing more intimate behaviour, it could not be assumed from this that they were gay. I did notice, however, that not one sympathetic local person I met in the gay bar or in public places could have been much over 25, which I found very intriguing.

Room service included by Vincent Norwich

I visited Tunisia in about 1965 with my partner Leslie. I had better explain to you that Leslie was a professional tour guide and so it was all part of his job that we went there. It was a fairly adventurous place to go in those days.

I think that in Hammamet when the locals saw two men together they guessed they would probably be available for friendship. For us it all seemed to revolve around the staff in hotels, especially waiters, who just couldn't have been friendlier and nicer .

We stayed first time in a very splendid hotel in South Hammamet called Les Orangers. The name was appropriate as there were orange or lemon groves all around it, between the hotel and the beach. On one occasion we went into one of the groves at night accompanied by two or three members of staff and had some fun and games together. I did not feel at all threatened or intimidated, although I think being away from the main harbour beach and in a quieter area may have been a help, as no one would have expected any naughties to be going on in that (South Hammamet) locality.

On one occasion we went to Douga, quite a well-known ancient site, and Leslie was listening to a lecture on tourism. I suppose I looked a bit bored, and one of the guides – who resembled Errol Flynn – signalled me to follow him (rather like André Gide's adventure in Sousse). He took me into a kind of tomb place and we had a gentle dalliance in there.

Back to Hammamet. There was a bar halfway between our hotel and the town, in quite an isolated area. It may have been called the Calypso but I am not sure after all these years. We would meet members of the staff there each evening and would often go outside for a session – my memory is that very little was ever done indoors!

We had become friendly with another gay couple at the hotel (we instinctively knew our interests were similar) and they used to come with us to the bar. Once we had a session near the Calypso where there were us four tourists and two or three members of the bar staff. One of the four tourists was a gay called William, a Scotsman who was in the theatrical world. It was almost his first time abroad and he was amazed and exhilarated by the whole business of being able to make friends so easily with the locals.

The little lane up to Les Orangers Hotel could also be fun and probably safer than the beach. When we came home from the bar, we would walk along the lane which had bushes on either side. Voices would come out of the bushes saying " 'Allo, monsieur. L'amour? L'amour?" We usually ignored them.

On our second holiday Leslie and I were back in Les Orangers but in one of the chalets out in the grounds of the hotel. We became very friendly indeed with the waiter who brought us our breakfast every morning.

The highlight of our second holiday (apart from the breakfast waiter) was when we went deep down into the south of Tunisia, to the town of Douz, from which we took a camel ride across the desert. We travelled down there at night on the bus and slept in the hotel down there, so we could start our desert trek first thing in the morning. I remember on the bus I sang a solo "Blue heaven and the stars up above!" from The Desert Song. It went down well with the passengers and seemed quite appropriate.

After the desert tour I did a slightly less ambitious tour on my own of the local minaret in Douz. One young Tunisian guide broke away from the main group, took me up a winding staircase and showed me his own (quite impressive) minaret.

Tourists in Tunisia being led (not astray we hope) by an Arab guide

For Leslie it was an important trip as he was researching for work as a guide and he could be paid quite good commission by the travel companies, so it was essential for him to build up his expertise. But of course my mind was free to wander a little and I did get up to a few things I must admit.. The only bad moment I had was when I saw a group of young men coming towards me and I remembered the film "Suddenly Last Summer" which I had unfortunately just seen before we left home. But in fact nothing happened.

Our breakfast friendship, by the way, continued with the waiter right up to the last day. Just before we left I gave him a dictionary as a present. He looked quite sad, as I was too. He came back a few minutes later, and with the sweetest of smiles gave me a gift in return. It was a sprig of jasmine ...

The smell of jasmine by *Ray Harvey-Amer*

Things began to change for ordinary folk in the Swinging Sixties. The mantra was "you've never had it so good". The economy was booming and attitudes changing. We had the birth and progress of the Black and Women's Liberation Movements, and amidst all this upheaval the emergence of a visible Gay Community that marched and defied societal conventions. It was the time when members of the Black, Female and Gay communities began to redefine who they were, rather than accept the labels previously applied by the establishment.

We also had more money in our pockets and were enjoying the blossoming changes to our lives and the economic freedoms that went with it. A side-shoot of this social revolution was the opening up of foreign travel for anyone who could raise the fare.

In 1966 Mike and I discussed taking a holiday somewhere in the Mediterranean. We noted that Court Airlines were offering a 2 week full board holiday in Tunisia for £65. This was a lot of money in the 1960s, but we managed to gather enough cash to book. Thus, in May 1966, with water-purifying tablets and high hopes of a holiday with a difference, we caught our plane at Luton Airport and flew south.

We landed at Tunis Airport, which had previously been a military airstrip – the buildings were relics of WW2. But beyond this first impression were the welcoming smiles of young men (at that time the women were very much hidden from view). It was the smiles and the sun of North Africa that immediately made one feel different from home.

Once through the hub-dub of customs and immigration, we were boarded onto a battered ex-military bus. Then through rutted and uneven roads we headed along the coast to Hammamet., observing through dusty windows as we went the orange, lemon and olive groves. And as we progressed along this bumpy route and as the light faded the perfume of jasmine entered the bus – it pervaded my soul and has remained with me ever since.

We arrived in Hammamet, then a small fishing village, two hours later. We were accommodated in bungalows. They were very basic with mattresses on brick plinths, a shower, loo, a washbasin, a mirror and a shelf. The swimming pool and dining area being central to the complex, which then opened onto a beautiful sandy beach. And all for £65.

A general view of the Hammamet corniche (Photo by Vincent Norwich)

I suppose Hammamet was then like the Spanish Costas before they were developed – in other words traditional and little changed since the 1930s. We had an exciting holiday and, with the locals, celebrated the acceptance of their New Constitution drafted by Tunisia's first President, Habib Bourguiba. It was a secular constitution which promised democratic rights for all Tunisians.

The locals were attentive and friendly, attention-seeking and strangely attracted to our shoes! But they also offered other favours for a few dinars. The hotel Residence Hammamet, was a popular place for queens and in those days I think you could book a room there for an hour if you ever felt the need. Some of the rooms had kitchen facilities. There was also a bar called La Brise, in the Avenue de la Republique but close to the Medina, which was an easy place for meeting young Tunisians, who would just stop and chat while you had your drinks outside.

But really you could meet the locals outside any café or bar and they seemed to love any opportunity for contact in those days. I think there was also a tradition of European men going out there in pairs – and of course if the locals saw a couple of Western men together, they got the message quickly.

They tended to come from big families and just enjoyed the attention. I am sure also that, even though tourism hadn't started in a big way, there was a long tradition in Hammamet, going right back, of making friends with visitors from other lands. I'd call the locals, at that time, amazingly helpful, nice and available when needed.

My next recollection of Tunisia was when the Croydon Gay Tennis Group chose it as a destination for one of their away tennis holidays. This must have been in the 1980s. We stayed in a much changed Hammamet, at the Hotel Bel Azur.

During the intervening period many hotels had been built. The fishing village was now much reduced and the way of life changing. But the smiling faces remained, and the smell of jasmine still filled the evening air. The thing that remained constant was those who wanted to a make friends and a few dinars around the town.

At the Hotel Bel Azur, I remember the queens who were already staying there would always have their dinner early so they could rush down to the cafés to see what was available, as the locals seemed always to go to bed early. I think most, or certainly a lot, of the fun and games happened in a Hampstead Heath type of way in the open air, maybe even on the beach.

But the most memorable episode of this visit was Mike winning the Inter-Hotels Tennis Tournament. I have the large Tunisian vase presented to Mike, in pride of place in my home[3].

---

[3] We look forward to hearing about Ray's (and also Vincent's) later Hammamet holidays further on, in Chapter 13.

6
The Baroness and Sir Roland
by Tim Vaughan

Jim Barron has sadly passed away and is much missed. He was only an occasional visitor to Tunisia, but he made his mark. His nickname was inevitably "The Baroness", yet with his loud, jovial and booming voice he was a male, assertive baron, with a great sense of fun and kindness. It was typical of Jim's humour and openness, by the way, that he told me his main Hammamet story, at the end of this chapter, "against himself" – most people would have kept quiet about it.

Back in Blighty, Jim was a real-ale fanatic and visited all those real ale festivals starting in the 1970s. He had, unsurprisingly, a large belly, so that with his big bushy beard, huge smile and baggy khaki shorts he was almost the archetypal real ale type, it even being said (untruly) that one real ale brewery had used his face as their emblem.

Jim's look-alike, advertising a brewery

One thing he did like towards the end of his life was the advent of Wetherspoon pubs, where he could obtain many varieties of beer cheaply. He introduced me to one in South London, which he told me was *not* the greatest of their pubs, although he insisted that we try each of the five types of real ale on display. By the end of the evening we'd both decided it was the best pub in London.

In fact all of the Baroness's interests seemed to begin with the letter b – another one being buses. He had started his working life as a bus conductor in Leeds and spent a lot of his time in later life campaigning to get both real beer and real buses (of the open-back, conductor-driver type) brought back. The very last time I met him, we took a ride on top of an old London routemaster bus on route thirteen, making one of its own final journeys from Baker Street down to Charing Cross

By this time his health was seriously failing, and when we reached a Wetherspoons pub in Whitehall overlooking St James Park for a little light refreshment, he told me that he no longer felt up to travelling in planes. "But, good news," he said jokingly. "I've heard they're extending bus thirteen through to Hammamet!"

I had to admit it was a nice idea.

Flashback: When Jim had first gone out to Tunisia around 1990 (by plane rather than bus 13), his travelling companion had been a charming and long-suffering gentleman from up north who was given by friends the special title of "Sir Roland", since he deserved a knighthood for working so hard protecting the Baroness. They were a delightful couple, although when they went on their travels together more than one person noticed similarities to Laurel and Hardy. ("Well, that's another fine mess you've got us into, Jim!").

Sir Roland had taken all his previous holidays in Scarborough but Jim had persuaded him to take his first holiday abroad now with him in Tunisia. Sir R. found all foreign ways and food unappealing, and he was not at all helped by a taxi journey from Monastir airport to Sousse. (They had decided to stay for a night or two at Sousse's Hotel de Paris in the Medina before continuing to Hammamet later.)

On their way to the Hotel de Paris, however, to Sir Roland's astonishment the taxi-driver announced to them firmly "I know why you English come to Tunisia – and here it is!" He unzipped his flies and (even more firmly) released his king-sized weapon, which neither of the travellers had any great desire to see just then.

Sir Roland was now wishing he'd gone to his usual b&b in Scarborough, and even the Baroness wondered what would have happened if they'd taken the taxi, as originally planned, all the way to Hammamet. (Perhaps "all the way" would have described it well.)

They much enjoyed, however, their day or two at the Hotel de Paris, set just inside the walls of Sousse's ancient medina. They became friendly with the two brothers working as both waiters and as bedroom-tidiers, or whatever the male equivalent of chamber-maids is. Sir Roland was worried about Jim drinking too much, so at the hotel's little restaurant downstairs, Restaurant du Peuple, he was very relieved to find that Jim was unable to purchase alcohol, with Muslim rules in place. Mind you, he did become suspicious about Jim's bottle of coke which he took down to dinner. It seemed to be almost the colour of red wine. How odd.

As soon as they arrived in Hammamet by train, Sir Roland was to spend half his time there trying to find a branch of Kentucky Fried Chicken and the other half trying to keep Jim out of trouble. Sadly he failed completely in the first mission and was fairly unsuccessful in the second, as our concluding story illustrates.

Having left Sir Roland back at the Hammamet hotel, still feeling nervous after that taxi journey, the Baroness met a very pleasant young friend selling flowers. (A local tradition, with some cynics saying it was just a chance to chat to foreigners, the flower often having lost most of its petals and being almost a stalk). The flowerseller's name was Abdul, and with a big smile he enthusiastically informed Jim that, if he wanted to get to know him better, they could rent a certain room for an hour in the village.

Jim called round at the given address and was very pleased to find that the lady of the house spoke extremely fluent French, as he did himself. He told her that he needed to hire the room for just one hour so he could have a rest away from the sun. The lady was very pleased to agree to all this and tactfully disappeared into the back of the house, while Jim took over the front room downstairs.

Jim then opened the window and signalled to Abdul, who had been discreetly but very excitedly waiting on the other side of the street, to come in. Closing the door, he quickly explained in sign language to Abdul that he wanted to give him the benefit of his renowned oral skills, and the lad was by this time almost beside himself with enthusiasm. So enthusiastic was he, in fact, that the whole thing came to a head much too quickly – one might almost say 'prematurely'. Abdul was embarrassed, but Jim assured him that it didn't matter and that he would definitely like to remain friends. Perhaps another day? So Abdul departed quietly but happily – while Jim decided, as he had nothing else to do, to go into the back of the house and practise his superb French on the charming lady.

Tapping on her door and being invited in, he proceeded to give her such exquisite French as "Enchanté, madame! Merci de faire votre connaissance. Je suis reconnaissant de toutes vos gentillesses."

She replied "De rien, monsieur. Moi aussi, enchantée ! Je suis de ma part très reconnaissante de vos gentillesses, aussi."

There then followed a round of French 'politeness' phrases :
"Merci mille fois." "De rien!"
"Enchantée, monsieur." "Enchanté, Madame."
"Il n'y a pas de quoi !" "Je vous en prie!"

Sensing this could go on all day, Jim gave a couple more "Enchanté-madames," and walked backwards to the door, bowing graciously as a final proof of how genteel he was.

Or so he thought. He was deeply shocked, however, on getting back to his nearby hotel room and looking in the mirror, to see that his bushy brown beard was still covered in something which should have been wiped away much earlier in the proceedings. (In football terms we might say that an over-enthusiastic player had shot wide of the goal mouth.) So perhaps the lady hadn't been quite as enchanted with his gentility as he had thought.

Still – although Jim had been left with egg on his face (or something similar), at least he now understood why the delightful lady hadn't given him the traditional French cheek-to-cheek embrace.

7
Short Tunisian Tales

First tale: Commuting Problems
by Charles Naden

In the 1970s I had a job very vaguely attached to the British embassy in Tunis, which meant I had diplomatic number plates. A mixed blessing.

Myself and my friend David used to go into Hammamet when we had any spare time, since the young Tunisians there were so friendly in those days and it was less than an hour away.

Hammamet

On one occasion, however, we had had no success meeting any friends at all – mainly because it was raining and Arabs tend to stay indoors when the weather is poor. On the way back, when David was driving, we noticed a young local who looked like a drowned rat by the side of the road. He cheered up enormously when we stopped to offer him a lift into Tunis and he was very relaxed, asking us where we were from, would we like him to show us round the ruins – all the usual small talk.

By this time it was dark and I noticed that David's driving was getting erratic, although I didn't attach much significance to it.

However during the journey I put my hand gingerly back towards the passenger to find out "is that a pencil or are you pleased to see me?" if you get what I mean. But as I homed in on the desired object, to my surprise my hand closed around someone else's hand…

Yes, David had got there first and, with him having only one hand on the wheel, it was a wonder we hadn't finished up in a ditch!

Hammamet's medina taken from the harbour beach outside.
(The swimming gear shows it was taken some time ago.)

On another occasion I drove on my own into Hammamet and met the most charming and attractive lad along the sea front, although his attire was more than a little scruffy. I just couldn't wait to get back with him to our flat in Tunis and I think my ardour got the better of me because I was driving too fast. Suddenly I was being waved down by a policeman in a restricted area and I saw I was in an embarrassing situation. I stopped. He walked slowly round the car.

"Ah," he said, viewing my number plates. "You from British embassy?"

"Yes," I replied meekly.

"And this?" he said, pointing to the dishevelled lad in the front. "This the British ambassador?"

Laughs all round and payment of an only slightly larger fine than usual – and off we went on our way, feeling very relieved.

2nd tale: *Getting the red light* by *Adrian Hammond*

Sandy Chester, one of the youngest of the travelling gentlemen featured in this epic, had not visited Sousse before but had (probably unwisely!) agreed to join Tim Vaughan during one of his stays there.

One day they decided to have a good look round the Medina. As they walked around the inner perimeter of the ancient Medina, the two travellers quite accidentally (or so Tim tells me) wandered into the notorious red light district. This was almost unique in the Arab world – a small area reserved for ladies of the night, providing services for heterosexual gentlemen. Most of the ladies, standing at their doors smiling and beckoning, were of a buxom nature and wearing the compulsory fishnet tights.

Young Sandy, having made the grievous mistake of entering, decided to speed through as fast as he could ahead of Tim, sadly not realising that the far end finished with a bend, a small pond and a wall (in that order). As he was reaching the bend which led to the pond/wall, a buxom fishnetted lady rushed to her door, calling out, "Terminée monsieur! Terminée!" Meaning that the street was coming to an end.

Sandy, however, thought she meant her last appointment was terminated and she was now free to give him her full attention.

"Non, merci, Madame. Non!" cried Sandy, in fear of losing his virginity and now starting to run.

"Terminée, Monsieur! Terminée!" cried the helpful lady, realising what would happen and running after him.

"Non, merci, Madaa– aaaaaagh..." cried Sandy, as his feet reached the oozing mud of the pond.

We are not going to exaggerate the story (now do we *ever* exaggerate?) by saying that Sandy was dragged from the depths of the pond by five fishnet-clad ladies, all screaming with a mixture of anguish and delight. Enough to say that both Tim and Sandy escaped from this doubly dangerous experience with their physical safety and their moral integrity completely intact. Or so Tim tells me.

That evening the two travellers, still in a state of shock after their visit to the red light district, had dinner in a recommended restaurant named 'Barakas', on the outskirts of Sousse.

Apparently the name has a historical tinge since 'Baraka' means 'a kind of religious good luck.' It was believed that a saintly man (source: the Encyclopaedia of Homosexuality) could 'transmit some of his baraka to other men by the mechanism of anal intercourse.'

After the excellent meal, however, Tim decided *not* to ask the very friendly, really rather saintly, manager why he had chosen that particular name for his restaurant. They had had enough new experiences for one day.

Sousse's medina from outside, with top of Hotel de Paris just showing.

The third, fourth and fifth short Tunisian tales in this chapter are by Brendon Knight, a veteran of Tangier (who will give us a tale of that city in Chapter 27).

Third tale: Something fishy

I did warn my newcomer friend to Sousse that he must watch out for thieving with the lads – but I'm afraid he had to learn the hard way.

He invited two locals round for supper and perhaps something else. He left one of them listening to music in the front room, while the other one helped him in the kitchen to cook up a piece of fish in a pressure cooker, then the fashionable means of cooking.

The music stopped and he thought the cassette needed changing, so he went back into the front room – where he found to his horror that his whole stereo system had been stolen! He raced out of the front door, just in time to see the youth on his bike wobbling away into the distance and carrying the stereo.

He tore back into the back of the house to get assistance from the other lad – only to see that one disappearing over the garden fence, with the pressure cooker – and his piece of fish in it.

Fourth tale: What a Sacrifice!

Another friend decided to move house within Sousse and got a local firm to help him with the removals.

He was more than a little surprised to see the furniture van coming down the street with his sofa on top – and on top of the sofa a sheep chained up and staring at him expectantly! The manager explained it was the local custom to sacrifice a sheep when you moved into a new house and he had decided to include the sheep – at no extra cost, he emphasised.

Despite the generosity of the manager my friend declined his very kind offer.

"I must say," said my friend "that the sheep looked very happy and comfortable sitting on my sofa – for one mad moment I thought of making him into a pet. Maybe I should've done."

Fifth tale: Oh, well!

Two gentlemen in Sousse became friends with two local brothers, and they passed a very pleasant holiday with them, finding them (astonishingly and strangely) undemanding about money/presents.

Towards the end of the holiday one gentleman said to the other "You know the whole thing is too good to be true – I think they're planning something – in fact I can feel a funny atmosphere building up whenever we see them."

He was right. A few days later the two brothers came round, sat at the kitchen table and started to sob and wail, with their hands reaching up to heaven and then their faces buried in their hands. "What on earth's the matter?" asked one of the gentlemen in French;

"C'est papa. Il est mort, il est mort, il est mort!" cried the older of the brothers. (Sob, sob)

"Oui," agreed the younger brother, "il est mort !" (Sob, sob, wail, moan)

"He is dead ?" asked my friend. "But when did he die?"

"Two days ago… but we cannot bury him!"

"You cannot bury him, but why ever not?" (As readers know, Muslims have to bury their dead quickly).

"Because papa, he fall in well and he drown!" explained the younger brother, letting out a very deep and expressive wail/sob.

"But I don't understand why you can't bury him."

"Because," explained the older one, who had at last stopped wailing, "papa at bottom of well and it cost 600 dinars (300 pounds) to get him dug out."

There was a pregnant pause…"What advice you give us?" asked the younger one, who had also stopped wailing and was watching the two gentlemen's reactions carefully.

"Well," said the more astute of my friends. "If I were you, I wouldn't drink the water."

Editor: Brendon, the writer of "Oh, well!" never met Albert, the writer of our next (final) short tale, but readers will notice an odd coincidence with the two tales.

Final tale: A trip to Mahdia
by Albert Bleesdale

Albert has sadly now passed away, but we are glad to be able to include his story about Tunisian holidays, before his Agadir days.

In the 1970s I had a very enjoyable holiday with my mother in Hammamet in Tunisia. Whilst there I met a charming young friend named Ben who came from the town of Mahdia. Eventually I got him a visa to come back to England where he worked with me in the pub trade and where we remained friends.

After four years, however, he decided to go back to Mahdia and open his own restaurant. We all arrived back at Monastir Airport together, but then I went one way with Mother to stay again at our favourite hotel in Hammamet, while Ben went off the opposite way to Mahdia to sort things out.

Now in those days Mahdia and Hammamet were connected direct by rail – the train went right through the middle of Sousse and then through Monastir.

Sousse's main square, with a train going through, and with a boat just in view in the harbour behind, c.1980

A few days later, however, I had a dramatic phone call at the hotel from Ben. He said I must go over to Mahdia immediately, because his mother had just fallen down a well! I had to take the train to Mahdia where he would send a taxi to the station to meet me.

I think my curiosity got the better of me – even though I had my doubts about the whole thing. So I caught the next train.

When I finally arrived at Mahdia station, to my surprise I saw that instead of a taxi there was a camel there to greet me! – with a "driver" who said he was from Monsieur Ben. He wanted to take me somewhere, and said something about "biïr". (At first I thought he wanted a beer, but then I remembered "biïr" is Arabic for a well.) I'll swear that camel was winking at me as if he knew what his master was up to.

But Mahdia station is in the centre of the town, and although I rather liked the camel I felt I would look a right wally riding on it – especially as I was wearing my best suit, thinking I might be attending a funeral. So I made an excuse about meeting a friend for lunch.

During lunch in a restaurant on my own I decided that rather than going straight back home I would get to the bottom of the story (if not of the well) and would hire a car to see what was happening. So I drove out to Ben's family house, which I had visited once before so I could just about remember where it was.

The next 2 photos are by Vincent Norwich:

Mahdia is built on a headland, with views over the sea to the south...

.....and views over the sea to the north

When I got to his house, the first thing I saw was his mother sweeping the path. She was looking extremely well considering she'd been down in the depths! Ben came out looking very sheepish, and no sign of the camel anywhere.

He explained that they'd managed to get his mother out of the well...but while I was there could we discuss the finances of his new restaurant?

I eventually got back to my hotel in Hammamet, where Mother and myself enjoyed the rest of our holiday – although I told the hotel not to put through any more calls from Mahdia.

Ed. There is another tale about Albert in Chapter 32 in the Tangier section.

8
A hotel to remember
by Tim Vaughan

Two views of the Sousse centre

I visited Sousse briefly in the late 1980's, staying at first in the Medina at the Hotel de Paris, just inside the ramparts. Not long after, however, I graduated to a more suitable one just outside the Medina called the Hotel de Rome, where it was possible in those days to "take back" the locals with whom you had become friendly.

In fact the hotel was a delightful place to be staying in. Downstairs there was a bar which, by the time I stayed there, had been turned into a kind of waiting room – one or two young locals would be sitting there, ready to catch the eye of any of the residents who might want to take them up to his room. They were always impeccably behaved, so that an irritating youth who had been following you round town would be sitting in the waiting room of the hotel as if butter wouldn't melt. Indeed if he had misbehaved he would have been quickly sent packing by the manager.

And on the subject of packing, or rather unpacking, one of the young locals' jobs was to carry newcomers' bags up to their rooms, as the lift was rather conveniently never working. On arrival in your room a few winks and nudges could be exchanged, and the lads were under no obligation to go back downstairs immediately, although they'd have already handed in their cards to the reception — to prevent theft and to prove they were at least eighteen.

Breakfast time at the Hotel de Rome was very convivial, since the place would be full of single gentlemen, happy to discuss their adventures and interests over boiled eggs and English tea. One morning I was eating my breakfast when I was both surprised and delighted to see a friendly Welshman named Cecil Bonneville walk in. We had last met on the Boulevard in Agadir the previous year. [4]

I would say there were few places in either Tangier or Agadir quite so relaxing as the Hotel de Rome, where friendships could be formed between gentlemen and other gentlemen, or between gentlemen and players, with such ease.

Sousse: a view of the historic port and medina.

I do remember one slightly embarrassing incident during a stay at the Hotel de Rome. I was having a pleasant holiday, doing a little research work as well as relaxing. Photocopying shops had just arrived in

---

[4] There is more on these coincidences in Chapter 10.

Sousse, and I called into one to do some copying. It was run by a most helpful lady who wanted to assist in any way she could.

While she was helping me, the door at the back of the shop opened and a stunningly beautiful boy of late secondary school age entered. It goes without saying that I wasn't interested in taking back such a young one. (I couldn't have got him back into the Hotel de Rome even if I had been.) But, in the words of the old proverb, "a cat may look at a king."

The lady excused herself and asked me if I would mind waiting while she got him organised for his new term at college, with folders and so on. Naturally I had no objection. After the lad had got his stationery together and had trotted off to college, I complimented the mother on her son's good manners (so much better than English boys, I said), and then asked how old he was.

"Sixteen," replied the noble dame.

"And what's his name?" I asked.

"Fatima," she replied.

Seeing my face fall, the lady laughed and said, "Yes everyone think she my son. She like wear jeans and play football with boys."

I was at a loss for words and felt it wiser not to ask if Fatima had any brothers.

Seeing my awkwardness, the lady said with the sweetest of smiles, "You are staying at Hotel de Rome?"

P.S. I visited the same shop several years later and saw some photos of international women's football games and teams on the wall. The same very charming lady told me that her daughter had become part of the Tunisian national women's football team!

9
Meeting new friends
by Tim Vaughan

(I have gathered the following from various sources, some from gentlemen who knew Sousse much earlier than I did himself.)

There used to be a big concentration of older European gentlemen in Sousse. There were several focus points in the 1980s – the most obvious being the very long seafront called the Corniche, where young males would sit nonchalantly, often in pairs, along the wall waiting to meet a European. They would also walk up and down the main Avenue Bourguiba, seeing who was sitting in the gentlemen's most popular daytime cafés – La Sirene (French word for Mermaid), Café Palace by the cinema, and Claridges, the longest established.

Earlier than that, up to the 1980s, I am told the best daytime place for meeting and making Tunisian friends had been the triangular jetty called Nahrawessa which jutted into the sea at the end of main Avenue Bourguiba. In the middle of it, behind Café Sirene, was an open-air café with a footpath all around the outside. The gentlemen would sit in the café drinking endless cups of coffee and the young men would walk all around, thus allowing everyone a second look, first from one side then the other.

Unusually for an Arab town, however, contact was often made in bars, which meant that younger ones were excluded, and those bars often featured dancing later at night. Around 1990, at the harbour/main-square end of the Avenue Bourguiba and opposite the municipal theatre, the principal bar was called the Café Tunisia, a huge establishment, now replaced by an even huger tower block. At the back of the Café Tunisia was a convenient entrance/exit to the street leading to the station. Wilber remembers there was a lot of coming and going through both exits, and a lot of drinking and dancing going on in a relaxed way between Tunisian males and Europeans (Tunisian females were never seen in bars).

A couple of comments about the Sousse cafés and bars. Firstly the management was often only vaguely aware of what was going on and didn't really connive in anything. For example, Claridges was almost a gay bar, although a quiet one without dancing. But even though it was a hotel as well as a café, there was *no question* of a European, having met someone nice downstairs, then renting a room for an hour's nooky upstairs. Secondly, as in Tangier, the most popular bars, would often change round, so a bar like Monkees might become less the "in place" if things had got too open and outrageous – with the alcohol having encouraged the younger element to get too boisterous and the management clamping down.

For example, a popular bar was at one time the Sousse Azur, vaguely in the centre of the district (the beach end of the main Avenue) where most of the "contact" cafés and bars were. It had a quiet and respectable café downstairs and, less conspicuously, a rather raunchy bar with a sea view upstairs. But in fact things had got so raunchy that the management decided to ban some European men, as they were tired of all the goings-on between them and the lads up there. (In Agadir the *lads* would have been banned.)

Sousse Azur bar (right), just off the beach end of the main Avenue

At one time, another of these Sousse contact bars became known as "Monkees" appropriately enough, although the entrance outside said something different. It was one of the oldest bars in the town, and at the height of its popularity Monkees would have music and dancing every night across both floors until quite late, with both groups of men, Tunisian and expats, joining in. Outside, in the rather quiet side-street, there could be one or two young Tunisians too, not entering because they had been banned or were a bit too young, hoping they'd make a last minute friendship with an expat leaving.

This quiet side-street led one way down towards the sea but the opposite way over a hill (probably the same hill on which the young André Gide had had his first gay experience many years earlier). The hill would take you by a shadowy and discreet route, with someone in tow, back to the main part of the town where you had your base – maybe a flat or maybe the Hotel de Rome.

Brendon Knight [5] who would often be seen in the cafés, had been a veteran of Tangier before deciding that Sousse was the best place for his holidays. He was in fact one of three gentlemen in Sousse who coincidentally all had long blond hair.

Another of the three blondes, with the surprisingly Arab sounding name of Yoosef, was noted for his superb dancing skills – with a hooker pipe in one hand, he would dance erotically with the local males to the music at Monkees or at Justinians, with both expats and local young men watching in genuine admiration. During the day he would sometimes don a long black thobe (Arab robe), but with his blond hair it was not quite clear if he was an Arab dignitary or an Anglican clergyman. But either way it had a dramatic effect.

Did Yoosef speak with a slight Arab accent or not? – no one was quite sure. Some tried to find out his origins but no one could quite solve the mystery, and that was just how Yoosef liked it to be.

Yoosef was held in respect by both Tunisians and British alike, by the former because of his supreme self-confidence and superb dress-skill, so that they held him to be a person of great importance and would often bow to him when they saw him. And by the latter as they were awed by the amount of money he seemed to have. On one occasion, I am told by a very reliable source, he drove up to Claridges in Sousse for afternoon tea. He was driving – wait for it – a brand new Rolls Royce, parking it casually and walking in for tea as if this was completely normal and in no need of explanation.

---

[5] Brendon has very interesting contributions in Chapters 7 and 27

Another regular on the scene, and friend of both Yoosef and Brendon, was a convivial and sociable Scot named John McGregor, who kept things together in the evenings amongst the regulars, in rather the same way as Cedric Singleton did during the day in Agadir. He was a retired Scottish dancing teacher, and he was able to get on well with everyone, which was no mean achievement.

"Come on now," he'd say at the Café Palace around 8.30, "Which dancing bar are we going to tonight? Shall it be Justinians?"

A further coincidence with John of Sousse and Cedric of Agadir was that they were both very interested in professional dance – John with Scottish and Cedric with traditional ballet.

Ed: Cedric was indeed the central figure in the expat scene in Agadir. He made sure everyone met together in the right café/restaurant at the right time, so enabling everyone to make new friends more easily.

He has written his memories of the Agadir scene, and these will be the central part of our, hopefully, next volume to be called "Agadir To My Heart." So here, to finish this chapter, is a photo of that friendly resort, with its old promenade and its Kasbah up high.

10
Meeting old friends
by Tim Vaughan

Sousse: Nahrawessa triangle (jutting out right)
marks the end of the 2-mile beach and corniche

I was having a holiday in Sousse when I began to realise that quite a few of the silver-haired gentlemen of Agadir had arrived there, although not commuting via Algeria as a general rule.

During this particular stay I remember walking along the corniche early one evening when I was very pleased to come face to face with an old acquaintance named Wilber, completely by chance. He was a pleasant Irishman, a friend of Albert, whom I had last met only a few months before at the Hotel Oasis in Agadir, also completely by chance. Whilst there we had attended a wonderful New Year's Eve party given for guests and staff, and had both been flirting with the younger waiters.

But even more old friends were there in town too, on that memorable Sousse holiday. Afternoon tea for the gentlemen in Sousse would usually be outside, and so I made a special point of asking Wilber to join me for tea outside Claridges the day after we had happily renewed our acquaintance. When we had both arrived there the next day we were pleased to meet the resident twins named Bert and Edgar, a charming couple whom I had first met for tea at Navarro's in Agadir! Always well-dressed and fashion-conscious, they were on this occasion wearing a pirate style head-scarf tied back in a bow, very much tying in with Sousse's pirate tradition.

Enjoying the company of Wilber and the twins, I decided to order a second tea and was then pleased by the arrival of Terence Riley, another regular from Agadir. He was a popular and jovial figure, with a pony fringe and florid complexion, who was known to many as The Empress Teresa and who used his organisational skills in London running a very successful gay social group .

It was not quite clear why Terence had decided to come to Sousse rather than Agadir this year. One version of the story was that the Agadir expats had become angry with him for giving them all female names and had decided to run him out of town. But the second version was almost the opposite – that he himself had become tired of people teasing *him*. This campery was said to have reached its climax in a juvenile campaign to get him to cover his very distinguished silver hair with a blue rinse, still popular amongst Tory ladies in those days.

A simpler explanation was his appreciation that in Sousse, unlike Agadir, you could drink beer in most of the open-air cafés. He was not alone in this appreciation, one has to admit.

With Terence, along came his companion Raymond King, yet another Agadir veteran and also an old friend of the twins, who was now giving Sousse a try. Raymond often added colour to the group with his striking dress sense, for example wearing pink trousers. Indeed, the conversation also brightened up too after he arrived, as he treated us to his stories of show biz in the past, when he had been a talented comic actor.

Raymond's only error, however, had been telling Terence and Tim how he had once played as a pantomime dame. He was instantly christened Widow Twanky. (An outsider might well comment that all this nicknaming would have made "The Fifth Form at St Dominic's" seem a model of maturity in comparison.)

Now that we were all gathered at Claridges café, cups of tea were replenished with hot water, and beer glasses filled. Conversation went on – a mixture of gossip about Agadir back in the good old days and Sousse as it was now:

> "Is it true xxx likes them to give him a good beating?"
> "Oh no, she's much too lady-like for things like that."
> "Well, I heard it on good authority."

And so on, and so on.

As we chatted, a good looking young Tunisian, strolling casually past, gave us all a knowing wink. Yes, life in Sousse life was very agreeable, we thought, and was never going to change.

But perhaps we were wrong.

General view of Sousse from main square, with Kasbah high in distance

11
Sousse diaries: extracts

Don Pickerson now gives us an extract from his diary, recorded on the first day of his stay in Sousse one summer, he thinks around 1990.

It shows, as we will also find out in the Tangier section, that some gentlemen were not just wanting short term relationships but were often interested in the long-term welfare of their young friends.

Arrived at sunset. The corniche was full of local youths winking, calling out "Sex? Sex! Ha; ha ha!"

The brothers arrived and we talked about their futures. Found out that before Hussein arrived at their apartment he was always stoned or high on something and he only stopped smoking the stuff six weeks ago. That was why he looked so sad when I first met him while he was getting the stuff out of his system. Also explains why he still sleeps a lot during the day as he had got used to getting stoned and then snoozing. He used to spend all his money on hash, drinking in nightclubs, of which there are several in Sousse. Sounds rather familiar and something I did myself for years.

He has been hanging around with some loser guys. I hope B. will set him on the right track and inspire him to get a real job. Who knows? They are all so young and have so many chances ahead of them if they set themselves up now. I was so lucky that I gave up dope soon enough to go to university etc.

They need to see how short life really is. They still seem to think it is endless and they do not need to worry about it. Hope I can impress on them the need to start doing things now. Maybe I should ask them what life means to them.Ibrahim is sick of all my talking – he just wants to have sex!! I talk too much for him anyway.

Met John the Scottish, nice old boy at the Café Palace and he said he was having a quiet holiday. It was good seeing him again.

Now a diary entry by writer Jerome Santos. He says this is a cautionary tale for anyone tempted to take a stranger back to their private flat.

I am recording these distressing events soon after they occurred.

I have been enjoying a cultural holiday in Sousse, with my friend Max Swindon. I have chosen to be in the historic area of

Tunisia as I feel it will inspire me to write further pieces for my slim volume of poetry I hope soon to have published. Max is involved in his new book on the causes of the Carthaginian Wars. We only agreed to stay in Sousse as it would be cooler on the coast, and we are sharing a flat above a little café. It is near to the railway station, which is convenient for Max's visits to Old Carthage, near Tunis, and also for his archaeological trips to el Jem.

El Jem, near Sousse, has some fine Roman ruins

However, certain other aspects of Sousse's 'culture' has already become all too apparent to us. The whole of the centre of the town and main promenade seems to be filled with over-sexed and opportunistic young men, as well as with a large number of European gentlemen (not so young).

It seems to us that alcohol is making the situation worse, not just because the visitors are drinking too much but also because a few of the locals are inebriated by about 9 pm and keen for the visitors to buy them another drink. I myself am only interested in mature and permanent relationships, the wisdom of age having taught me to shun short-term friendships such as those on display here.

Max also very strongly disapproves of aspects of the Sousse scene, and especially of all the drinking. Unfortunately, however, there is one young man selling nuts down at Café Sirene (handsome with dark curly hair) who has managed to catch his attention.

This afternoon I was having my usual siesta when, unusually, Max knocked on my door and walked in before I was even fully awake. Behind him entered none other than the young nut-seller, whom I regret having to record was stark naked.

"I thought your holiday needed cheering up," Max said. "He's called Abdul Danees and he's keen to meet you."

I remember wondering why Max was passing him on to me, but Danees had only been in the room on his own for one minute when I perfectly understood. He was through all my drawers, trying out all the deodorants, squirting perfume all over himself and the furniture. He then picked up my camera and started taking snaps of his own rather large member, which seemed to be getting considerably larger as the camera went on clicking. (I must remember not to take that film into Guildford Boots to be developed.)

I had also left my wig beside the bed while I dozed. The moment Abdul Danees spotted this he became very excited and tried it on in front of the mirror. But much worse was to follow. Absolutely nobody could accuse me of not having a sense of humour, but there is nothing even remotely funny about Danees putting my wig onto his upright member and running naked round the flat. I remain justifiably furious.

By this time Max realised he had made an error of judgment, caught the lad and retrieved my wig. He spoke to the lad in Arabic explaining we would both give him a little 'floos' if he agreed to leave the flat immediately.

Thank God he agreed. And it is only since Danees departed that we have both noticed how apt his name is. Danees the Menace.

12
Under the jolly roger
by Crispin Arnold

I always used to enjoy travelling with my friend Sylvester, back in the late 1970s/early 1980s. We were a gay couple at that time yes, but we had an eye to something occasionally outside our relationship. Back in the 50s I suppose we would have looked for friendship with sailors and guardsmen in the UK, but of course those days had long disappeared even when this story happened.

On our first visit to Sousse we were much enamoured with the scene and by the large number of butch, hunky young locals who made it clear they were not averse to friendship.

Sousse harbour – photo taken surprisingly close to the main town square

One day we decided to visit the harbour area, at the other end of the main street. Perhaps the chance of meeting sailors – who knows? Along the harbour front we saw a number of huge boats tied up. I mentioned to Sylvester how my Uncle Bill had sailed from Sousse harbour during World War II, part of the very first allied spearhead into occupied Europe, bound for Sicily.

As we walked further along the port something even more historic caught both our eyes. Tied up at the far end were fabricated 'pirate' sailing boats – old-fashioned looking boats with modern motors which would take tourists for a 'sail' around the bay. The crew would be dressed up as pirates and during the voyage the passengers would be entertained by the crew with fire-eating, walking on nails or swallowing swords and so on.

But Sylvester was quite adamant that he wasn't going on a thing like that., saying it was contrived and childish. So there.

As we strolled along, however, two well-built and friendly members of the crew with bare muscular torsos, dressed in full pirate gear, walked toward us, smiling invitingly and suggesting we should have a quick look round the boat (no obligation of course). And once we had entered the boat we were given a great deal of special attention and seated down, both of us next to one of the two pirates who had invited us on board. Not much chance of escape now!

Sousse harbour again, with a pirate boat ready for action

Sylvester started to soften up in his views now he could see the pirates' muscles up close. He said something about how educational a tour like this could be, and adding how we both needed to get out and about more. Yes, well. So we were signed up to join the other tourists. The anchor was pulled up and the voyage began.

Not the ones in the story! A brave pirate gets ready to entertain the passengers, while the cabin boy claps out the musical rhythm

During the trip and in the middle of the fire-eating performance, with whispered conversations, Sylvester managed to persuade the two special pirates who had got us on board to visit us later on in our flat after the voyage. How *bold* of him.

To be quite honest I was filled with some fear about Sylvester's boldness, and wondered if we were taking a big risk. The two of them were much stronger than the two of us.

Anyway, the arrangement was that after the trip we would make our way to Café Cristal near the port, where the pirates would join us later, after they had done all their jobs with the boat. So an hour later, disembarking from the boat we pushed our way through the crowd of young flower-seller lads who always welcomed the boats back, and walked across the square to Café Cristal.

In fact we waited there a very long time drinking coffee, and we had almost given up hope, when to our great joy they suddenly arrived from the opposite direction (they had probably walked round in a circle), and nodded to us discreetly. We paid the bill and the pirates surreptitiously followed us back to the flat.

In the privacy of our respective bedrooms we found that they were much gentler and nicer than we had dared to hope. Mind you, I think Sylvester and I did keep up the fantasy of them being pirates and us being their wenches! We were, after all, now under the sign of the Jolly Roger and I suppose it's even possible that we were jolly-rogered – I really can't remember after all these years.

A pirate boat comes into port in Sousse

We would usually meet them at Café Cristal after their boat had come in, and we really thought that *our* boat had come in too. Our original fears were completely unfounded, because the two 'pirates', cousins named Faroush and Hammed, turned out to be both honest and affectionate. Faroush was usually with me in one room and Hammed with Sylvester in the other, and the double friendship, raunchy yet romantic, continued all through our holiday.

Of course all good things must come to an end, and so after ten days under the Jolly Roger, and with great reluctance, we had to say a sad farewell both to Sousse and our pirate companions. Sadly we never saw our two pirate friends again whenever we returned to Sousse – we would often walk along the harbour when the boats came back, hoping we might meet them.

But we never did.

The North African coastline from Tangier right across to Sousse used to be called the Barbary Coast and was famous for pirates

13
Later Tunisian holidays

Back in Chapter Five, Ray and Vincent gave us memories of earlier trips to Tunisia. This chapter gives us their recollections of later holidays there, about twenty years after.

Exploring the Deep South by Ray Harvey-Amer

Time had gone by since my first trips with Mike to Tunisia. We both pursued our careers. Mike in the business of painting& decorating and me in nursing.

My next visit to Tunisia was after Mike died. I was now 54 and needed to get on alone in my life. Perhaps it was that smell of jasmine that directed me back to Tunisia in the 1990s, although this time I wanted to explore new parts of the country. I think Mike would have approved.

I acquired a copy of 'Tunisia the Rough Guide', scoured its pages and plotted a course. First stop was the town of Sfax.

Sfax in the south of Tunisia

Then the Islands of Kerkennah. The islands are about one hour on the ferry from Sfax. The terrain is flat with thousands of palm trees. On arrival at Port Youssef, waiting were the buses and taxis ready to take locals home and the visitors to their hotels.

My hotel was Le Grand, and it would continue to be so for many years. Le Grand offered simple accommodation and cuisine, but was known for its beautiful location. (Panorama was the only tour operator and a devoted clientele of returnees had grown over the years). Women of a certain age were most apparent, as was their attraction to the young fishermen from Melita, a small village down the coast. The gay element was less apparent. Though those gays that did discover Kerkennah were to be pleasantly surprised at the satisfying attention they found in the locals, in a Querelle de Brest [6] kind of way.

My other discovery was the village of Douz situated on the edge of the desert. Douz is famous for two things. Firstly, as it is on the very edge of the Sahara, it's the starting point for camel rides out into the desert, often involving several days. Secondly, every December it's the setting for the Desert Festival – when there would be lots of parades, musical events, horse and camel races and so on.

Douz is the setting for Tunisia's Desert Festival

---

[6] Genet's novel about friendships with sailors

We used to go twice a year to Douz, once always for the Festival. Over a period of ten years I stayed at the hotel 'Rose des Sables', a time-warped edifice reminiscent of the 1930s. My first visit was with Doreen, a kind friend I'd got to know from my visits to Kerkennah and who reminded me slightly of Margaret Rutherford.

The Rose was situated amidst the palms just down from the open expense of the desert. It had been one of the first hotels built for tourists, but was now superseded by modern luxurious desert-side four star hotels. The Rose couldn't compete with them.

On our first visit we were charged for half board 15 dinars (£7.50). Then as time went by, and I returned alone without Doreen, who had sadly passed away, the price gradually reduced to 10, then 5 then nothing. To me the Rose des Sables offered something better and more genuine than the 4 star hotels. Even the grime and dust seemed to say "much has happened here". And the staff who over the years became my friends and lovers. They were always undemanding, sensitive and interested beyond the bed chamber.

I visited this idyllic spot for over ten years, got to know the people, to love their friendship and the beauty of their sons.

Keeping up appearances
by Vincent Norwich.

This was the first holiday that I had taken in Hammamet since my partner Leslie had passed away, and it took place around 1990. On this occasion I went with Tim Vaughan.

We had the usual problem of finding "sturmfrei" accommodation (in other words a place where you could take back a friend to your room without fear of a storm breaking out). We were staying in the Hotel Benila in the Hammamet South district, where "taking back" was impossible, but where we got to know a very respectable, friendly Irish lady and her daughter. Tim quickly found out that, like him, they were of a religious bent, and they were very impressed with his stories of pilgrimages to Walsingham, how he had once met the Bishop of Bath, etc, etc.

On our second afternoon, however, as we were trotting on our own along the sea-front, we saw another unmistakable figure striding towards us – tall, slim and with profuse snow-white hair waving gently in the breeze. It was our old friend, Jack Chatterton, often known as Lady Chatterley, waving and smiling at us cheerfully. He was delighted to see us both, as we him too.

We discovered that, although staying in a hotel, Jack did occasionally use a flat during the day. "Just to rest from the sun," he explained. "Well, I think the three of us should all partake of some tea and scones in The Cavern. And it's my treat!"

Now The Cavern was a café into which you descended from the harbour promenade down a very steep flight of steps. Its back opened onto the beach but it had a roof and was covered on three sides, making it cool in summer and warm in winter, so becoming a favourite gathering place for English fraternity.

Photo taken from a boat, showing Oscar's reputed house and with the dark beach entrance to The Cavern on right.

In fact it was currently being run by a gay couple, originating from Earls Court, called Norman and Trevor. (We nicknamed them Nora and Thelma.) They had put up an enticing sign at the top of the steps "Come down here and you'll find what you're dying for." Then in brackets, "A nice cuppa tea." The charming duo liked to keep up with all the local news, and made sure everyone else did too!

After Trevor had brought us in the tea and was bustling around with the scones, we sat drinking our cuppas in the cool shade of the Cavern and listening to Jack speaking with his exquisite manners. We began to realise during tea that, quite apart from his surname, the title of Lady Chatterley was fully justified,with phrases such as "How kind!", "Lovely to see you again," and "Would you be so good as to pass the sugar?" perforating the conversation. I think that Tangier in the old days had been called "an oriental Cheltenham," and there was no doubt about it – Jack was now bringing a touch of Cheltenham into Hammamet.

After a while, however, Jack announced that he needed to be off to visit the Charm Beach, about ten minutes away from the harbour beach we were currently on.

"I'm told it's sometimes used for assignations, being a bit off the beaten track," he explained. "But it goes without saying I'm not interested in things like that. Such lovely flowers and plants there."

When Jack had settled up the bill and was striding on his long legs across the sand towards the Charm Beach to inspect the exotic flowers, Norman/Nora bustled in to see if we needed extra scones.

But Jack has set our minds thinking about something else....

That very evening, well before it was dark, we felt it was time to explore the Charm Beach, mentioned to us by Jack over tea and our curiosity having been aroused.

As we were walking from the hotel towards the village, however, ready to turn off down to the beach, we came face to face with a friendly and handsome young local, quite tall with wavy hair and a lovely smile, named Aydee Mohamed. He quickly made it plain that he wanted to be our very special friend.

When we told him that sadly we had no apartment, he told us to have no fear and just follow him! Expecting him to lead us down to the Charm Beach, rather to our surprise he took us the opposite way across some fields and into an empty shepherd's cottage (he had been doing some farm work there), where we were all able to disrobe in a rather romantic setting.

"It's lucky those Irish ladies at the hotel can't see us now, isn't it?" I whispered during the performance.

"Ummm, yeah," said Tim who was licking Aydee's feet.

"Very biblical," I commented.

We found out that Aydee originated from outside Hammamet and had come into the town to find a job. His father had gone to Marseilles to work, leaving him partly responsible for his mother. I think he was keen to get to Marseilles himself eventually.

The friendship blossomed as these friendships do. We were able to find a very adequate apartment in a pleasant little complex on the Avenue de la Republique, near the Hotel Khella. It consisted of a number of small, almost bungalow-like, apartments facing into a central courtyard. (It was a complex, we noticed after a while, used by several other older and single gentlemen.)

Aydee would spend one night with Tim and the next with me, and so on – although we had kept our rooms at the hotel as they were part of the holiday package deal.

One morning at breakfast in the little bungalow/apartment, as we were munching our baguettes, we were unwise enough to tell Aydee we wouldn't be seeing him that day as we were going on the train to Sousse. Aydee jumped up and down with excitement, explaining that he knew Sousse like the back of his hand and he would be our guide!

So the three of us set off together for Hammamet's little station, looking forward to a lovely day out. On the station platform platform, whom should we meet but (you've already guessed) the two Irish ladies from their hotel – ooooh, dear!

The ladies were very pleased to see us and explained how they were going on the same train but their destination for the day was not Sousse but Sfax, since they had heard it was "the most beautiful city in the world." [7] But as the two Irish ladies finished their enthusiastic account of Sfax and we could hear the train hooting in the distance, their eyes fell on the third person in our party on the platform. "Is he going with you to Sousse too?" the ladies asked.

---

[7] The quote is from gay author Ronald Firbank but no one fully understands why he said it, although see the photo back on page 65 to judge for yourself

"Er, yes. He's our umm, guide," replied Tim.

An embarrassed silence now fell on the platform. We were relieved they were not going to the same destination as us, and Tim thought it best not to get back on religion again

Perhaps we were naïve. Anyone with experience of the Third World would guess what would happen when we arrived in Sousse. Yes, Aydee did indeed know a lot about Sousee but his knowledge seemed to be centred on the clothes shops in the Medina there. He took us into his favourite ones and found out how quickly he could empty our wallets. Luckily neither of us had credit cards, this still just about being in the days of travellers' cheques.

Arriving back somewhat exhausted outside Sousse's quite impressive main station, we looked up the hill – and to Tim's excitement saw a wonderful church spire in the distance at the top of it. Aydee told us he would love to show us the way up to it.

The spire turned out to be that of St Felix, I am told the finest church building in Tunisia apart from Tunis Cathedral.

St Felix Church in Sousse, set on a hill

"Well at least he won't be able to spend our money up there," Tim muttered, as we three pilgrims trudged up the hill together.

As soon as we entered the church we were met by a novice assistant priest, a Frenchman, and on this occasion Aydee had enough tact to fade away. Beginning at the altar, the young priest took us on a tour of the church, telling us anecdotes of its history. (I think the gist of it was that at one time a lot of French Catholics had lived in Sousse and they had found the money to build the church.)

We finished up twenty minutes later outside the church in the garden, from which he could show us the fine façade and describe the architecture in detail.

With Tim's confidence now fully returned, he told the priest about his church background and how he had met every other bishop in the western world, etc., etc. The Frenchman was indeed greatly impressed.

Having said our thanks and farewells to the young priest outside the church, we looked around for Aydee, thinking he was bound to join us again if only to get his train fare back. But where on earth was he?

The church door opened and the priest/guide said in a slightly cold tone of voice "Have you left something behind?"

Sheepishly we re-entered. The priest pointed to the high altar, where stretched on top and looking very comfortable, was young Aydee – having grown sleepy with all his shopping and with the sound of the voices, he was having a little snooze on the very best bed he could find.

(Vincent & Tim promise us the 'Aydee sleeping on the altar' story is true!)

14
Those sad eyes
by Sam Raynor

I was having a long lazy holiday in Tunisia with my very good friend Joe Rossiter one spring in about 1985, partly to celebrate my early retirement. We had chosen the town of Hammamet because of its association with André Gide and Oscar Wilde, whose houses (or the houses where they stayed) were on the seafront.

You ask me what Hammamet was like at that time? All I can say is there used to be numerous young males, aged between 14 and 40, everywhere you looked around the centre. They were relaxed and smiling, giving the impression they were pleased to see you.

Hammamet house (left) where OscarWilde is said to have stayed with Medina in the background

I have holidayed in the town recently and all of this seems to have now gone, with hardly any of the locals speaking to you and few taking any notice or interest in you, except sellers.

Of course even in those days they were, I think, discouraged from going to the tourist hotel area, which was about two miles from the village itself. But the village belonged then to the young Tunisians of very varied ages: sometimes the lads would be selling flowers in the street, or selling cakes on the beach – rather in the same way as many of them in Tangier used to be shoe-shiners – and they could often be drawn into conversation.

Back to my own holiday. One morning I had just gone to the bakers shop and was crossing the old bus station (which has now been turned into a market), my mind a thousand miles away as they say, when I felt someone catching hold of my sleeve and a soft gentle voice said "L'amour, monsieur?"

I turned round and there was the most handsome, cutest young companion you could wish to meet standing there. He was called Salha (short for Salhadin – you might just remember the name "Saladin" from your history lessons?).

Those sad eyes are what I most remember – there was always something just a little bit sorrowful about him, even in that very first greeting he gave me. I later found out that he had become very attached to a German tourist who had left without saying he was leaving or even saying goodbye, had just not turned up when he was expected, which isn't the way to treat anyone.

Salha came back to my flat straightaway, and then every day. In bed he loved doing it in a certain way, which perhaps he had learnt from the German – always from above, thrusting gently into my mouth, with his lovely smooth thighs astride me. Well, enough of that. Let's just say he became an all-time favourite, not only because of his exquisite body but because of his lovely personality too.

The only problem which arose with him really wasn't his fault – he had brought a friend back at my suggestion, on his second or third visit, so that Joe would have some company too, and this friend organised a bit of petty thieving in the flat. We got annoyed with both of them. (I'm afraid the Hammamet lads had a reputation for this, and even dear Oscar had had his problems with them.)

Anyway, we told them both to leave. However, Salha came round, full of apologies, begging to be re-instated, and my heart melted almost immediately. From then on I never had any problems with him at all. Joe had also found a more trustworthy friend by this time, a likeable and affectionate doughnut seller from the beach, named as far as I remember Fowzi.

I always managed to make contact with Salha when I returned to Hammamet. Often I could ask others, like Fowzi, if they had seen Salha, and they went and found him. Having an unusual name helped. (It was a hopeless situation if you'd fallen in love with someone called Mohamed – when you asked around, up to a dozen Mohameds could arrive.)

Hammamet beaches stretched for miles, with the
Medina in the distance and many salesmen around

On a later trip to Hammamet Salha invited me back to meet his mother – he was an only son and the father seemed to have deserted the mother to live in Tunis. His mother used to run a tiny sweet stall (from which I think Salha had most of the sweets when younger!).

When I went round for the meal I was made to feel very welcome – Salha explained that I could bring a gift if I wanted but it didn't matter. I decided to take some food and goodies around and they appreciated it. The evening went very well, except that his female cousins were making eyes at me as a potential husband.

Family in a different town: being invited back to meet the younger members of the family seems to have been a general Arab tradition.

Soon after this, back in London, I went down with a serious kidney illness and lost interest in both travelling and the other thing. One day I was lying in hospital in a light sleep, having I suppose got over the worst of the illness, and I dreamed that something was touching my lips from above, probably the blanket, which gave me a warm, comforting sensation. I realised it had reminded me of Salha, whom I am sorry to say I had almost forgotten during my illness.

I think that little erotic feeling helped me to get better and to want to get on with living again. It led me to deciding to go back to Hammamet to see if I could find Salha, with those sad eyes, again. So as soon as the doctors said I could travel again I booked my flight to Monastir — although it was a while since I'd been.

On arrival in Hammamet, I expected to find Salha again by asking around like I had before, but no one seemed to have seen him for ages. Finally I called round to see his mother, who could not have been more friendly but who said, "Salha habite a Tunis – il travaille."(He's living in Tunis, working).

Then it was my turn to feel sad.

Ed. As Monastir has appeared several times in these chapters, maybe we could give it the last "footnote" in this Part One of the book.

Monastir, 12 km to the south-east of Sousse, was noted not just for its airport but also as the birthplace of the first Tunisian president, Habib Bourguiba. It was a delightful resort in its own right, perhaps quieter and more relaxing than Sousse or Hammamet, and easy for the expats of Sousse to reach by metro. (There was always a slight mystery about why so many of its hotels were closed.)

Ron Nelson mentioned that its attractive rocky peninsula, at front of the photo, was known in past days as an occasional meeting point between locals and visitors.

This view of the pleasant resort of Monastir ends Part One of the book.

PART TWO:

TANGIER
THE IMMORTAL

15
Tangier, City of Freedom
by Tony Walton
The dream

Tangier was established long before Rome – sufficient to make it of huge historic interest. Moreover it is situated at the fulcrum of the world, a central point between Africa, Europe and America, and also between the Atlantic and the Mediterranean.

Many eminent writers visited it over the years, such as "The Three Musketeers" author, Alexander Dumas. And on his way from America to the Holy Land, the author Mark Twain visited Tangier in the late 19th century: it was perhaps appropriate that one of the great portrayers of the younger male (wicked but loveable) should have wandered down its streets – perhaps getting ideas for future "Huckleberry Finn" type of characters and their antics.

Disembarkation of passengers at Tangier port, c.1930

Yet it was during the time of the International Zone, 1920-1957, that Tangier came into its own. The two most comprehensive books on life in the city at that time are Iain Finlayson's "Tangier: City of the Dream", and Michelle Green's "The Dream at the End of the World." It's interesting that they both put the word "dream" into their title, and they both mention Paul Bowles' famous dream, of which more later in this chapter. The first person, however, to mention "dream" in connection with Tangier was not Paul Bowles but (believe it or not) St Francis of Assissi.

In the Middle Ages St Francis had apparently expressed his wish to organise a missionary journey to Tangier, condemning the behaviour of the city in the words: "O Tingis, Tingis, O dementa Tingis, O Moruecos, illusas civitas." (O Tangier, mad Tangier, O Moroccan people, living under a dream). Sadly, St Francis didn't provide further details of which particular things in Tangier were causing him such concern.

But as stated above, it was in the early twentieth century that Tangier became especially important, from both the literary and the gay viewpoint. Many have related how life sparkled there in a way it usually failed to do in the capitals of Europe during the years 1920 to 1960. Henri de Montherlant, for example, the author of several successful plays and novels, most with a gay theme, visited Tangier often and described it as "the white dove on the shoulder of Africa."

The Tangier International Zone, with its very vague and laissez-faire rule, often produced more freedom of expression, movement and sexuality during the 1940s/1950s decades than New York, London or even Paris. (Interestingly that other international city, West Berlin, also became a centre of liberalism, sharing some free 'n easy things in common with the Tangier International Zone.)

Another gay capital?

So it would not be much exaggeration to say that Tangier was virtually the gay capital of the world, taking over from Algiers, during the years when it was an international zone.

And it was in the last part of that period, following World War II, when it really came into its own, since that was an era of general gloom for gay people in virtually all the capitals of Europe and North America. (Paris was the least repressive of the capital cities and so, for example, the gay author James Baldwin settled there to escape from McCarthyist USA. But because of the Nazi/Petain wartime repression and its anti-gay legislation, which it took decades to get rid of, Paris failed to become again quite the same "gay Paree", in both senses, it had been between the wars).

So Tangier filled a very important gap during those years.

Café de Paris, 1950s. A Tangier meeting place, with view of harbour

The literati

Thus it is probably true that Tangier became the most free city in the world for gays. Yet there was another very significant aspect of Tangier – the fact there were so many *literati* amongst the expats inevitably meant that their lives and thoughts became thoroughly documented, and much more so than other cities, such as Tunis, which were well frequented by gays but sadly little documented.

From the 1920s, for example, intellectuals like the Americans Gertrude Stein and her lover Alice B Toklas had been seeking mental and emotional refuge in Tangier. Dividing their time between there and Paris, Gertrude Stein planned a short story whilst she was staying in Tangier called "Miss Furr and Miss Skeene." Published in Paris in 1922, it uses the word "gay" in its modern sense. People could argue about when and where the word was first used, but this is the first evidence of it in print. (Interesting that a term now used exclusively for male homosexuals was first used by and about female ones.)

A later example there of the many gay or gay-sympathetic writers was Alec Waugh, brother of Evelyn Waugh, who spent as much time as he could in Tangier in the 60s and 70s, visiting such places as the Café Central but also the more upmarket Madame Porte's. His book of most gay interest was "The Loom of Youth" which had taken the lid off English public schools friendships – to a generation brought up on the more naïve "Tom Brown's Schooldays". His other famous book "Island in the Sun" was made into a film, with the well-known song by Harry Belafonte.

Many intellectual gentlemen had gone to live in Tangier during those repressive 1940s and 1950s, forming a literary community there and desribing themselves as Tangerinos. The most important (in the sense that he became the centre of the community there) was the American writer and lyricist, Paul Bowles.

Bowles, who loved Tangier dearly, was Morocco's leading expat

Seeking to escape the restrictions of a USA dominated by the appalling McCarthy, in the early 1950s Bowles had visited many places in his quest for freedom. He had met Gertrude Stein in Paris and she had suggested he should try out Tangier, which he did.

However, he went on to visit several other places worldwide too. He explains in his memoirs how one night, whilst staying in Ceylon, he dreamed he was walking through the streets of a town – without knowing where it was and yet knowing it was the one place where he knew he belonged. On waking, Bowles realised that the streets he had been dreaming of were those of Tangier. Returning to that city soon after the dream, he was never again to abandon it, and becoming the central figure in the expatriate life there.

His most famous books are "Let it Come Down", "The Sheltering Sky" and "The Spider's Web." But his most homosexual story was probably "Pages From Cold Point" in which a boy tries to seduce his father. Bowles's wife Jane, also gay orientated and likewise an author, produced much less than her husband, although some critics think even more highly of her work. Her most famous pieces were "In the Summerhouse" and "Two Serious Ladies."

Another of the authors who took a house on the fashionable district known as The Mountain was E F Benson. There is in fact a theory that although the "Tilling" of Benson's well-known "Mapp and Lucia" stories was based ostensibly on Rye in Sussex, some of its characters may well have had their origins in the folk of the other orientation who lived in Tangier, because Benson certainly knew Tangier society extremely well, having been one of its expats.

The index of "Tangier, City of the Dream" lists, incredibly, over forty authors who lived or stayed in Tangier during its golden years. Apart from those already mentioned in this chapter (Benson, the two Bowles, Stein and Waugh) here are the other most famous: Djuna Barnes, William Burroughs, Truman Capote, Noel Coward, T.S. Eliot, Jean Genet, Ian Fleming, Allen Ginsberg, Richard Hughes, Henri de Montherlant, Joe Orton, Alan Sillitoe, Gore Vidal and Tennessee Williams. Many of these were gay or bisexually orientated.

In the period from the 30s to the 60s, the favourite place for several of them to gather was the bookshop called "Librairie des Colonnes" on Rue Pasteur, which was still there recently. Several of the famous writers were regular visitors to the bookshop (although apparently Jean Genet used it mainly to cash cheques!).

In fact, it was said that the three best places for the 'important' people to meet in Tangier were the Bowles' living room, David Herbert's dinner table and the Librairie des Colonnes.

A Tangier puzzle

Several books on Tangier mention that both Oscar Wilde and André Gide visited Tangier – usually they are thrown casually into a long list of the famous who went there in the past. It would be wonderful if they had done, being such eminent gays. However, we have looked at all the sources thoroughly (the Oscar Wilde Society has also very kindly investigated) but with regret no one can find any firm evidence of either of those two writers visiting the city.

In terms of likelihood Oscar is the *less* likely of the two, since he lived only until 1900 and was busy going to other exotic places. In the last few years of the 19th century, Algiers and Tunis were the places to go, so there wouldn't have been much incentive then for Oscar or others to make the longer journey across the water to Tangier. And Tangerino Croft-Cooke's book "The Unrecorded Life of Oscar Wilde" certainly makes no mention of a visit to Tangier.

Gide, on the other hand, lived until 1950 and by that time many of the literati had decided that Tangier was the "in" place to be. So although nothing is recorded, it would seem probable that Gide went there during the international zone years – if only to meet some of his literary friends. Certainly the story prevailed that a certain table in the Café Central had been reserved for him during the inter-war years, he being a familiar figure in cloak and large floppy hat. [8]

Other arrivals

For the less 'booky' expats, the cafés and bars were the other great meeting places, and one of our two historians, Paul Horler, will be mentioning the five most famous bars. The area of Tangier known as The Mountain had sprung up by this time, with fashionable and fairly large houses being built. Café society, both in the Petit Socco but also around the more upmarket Boulevard Pasteur, really thrived. But along with the cafés, several famous hotels were also built in the 1920s, most famously the Muniria. [9]

Many other less wealthy gay people had started going to Tangier after World War I, since it was not so far from Europe,

---

[8] see photos on pages 14 & 15

[9] see Chapter 23

either for a long holiday or on an expat basis. We say "long holiday" as most of them would have travelled by boat from Marseilles or from Southampton, long distance plane journeys for civilians not commencing, as you know, until the 1930s at the earliest, and even then would have been very expensive.

Later, Tangier became a kind of Mecca for the Beat Generation, including the more moderate aspects of it. The Rolling Stones, for instance, those symbols of 1960s adolescent rebellion, performed several concerts in Tangier, finding it a convivial place to be. Which reminds us that although the theme of this book is the large number of gays who went to Tangier at a time when gayness was against the law in Europe, there were also many straight people seeking different sorts of freedom there.

Financiers, for example, found the lack of monetary restrictions in the Zone very attractive, which itself served to create more prosperity there than in the surrounding areas. This prosperity encouraged young men outside the Zone to come into the city to seek their fortune, as well as to find more freedom.

Freedom – or maybe excitement? Such as Eddie Chapman, the real-life hero depicted in that wonderful spy/war film "Triple Cross", who found life so dull in England after the war that he went out to Tangier to organise smuggling runs between the zones!

High society

Of course not all the expats of Tangier (Tangerinos) were specially intellectual and one of the most famous who arrived in the 1960s, David Herbert, would not have described himself in those terms, although his autobiography "Second Son" is certainly well written.

Herbert, who was churchwarden of Tangier's Church of England (St Andrew's) for many years, liked to know everything that was going on, and when he talked affectionately about the "the old eccentric English, the old ladies" of Tangier, it's not completely certain which gender he was referring to. He was the second son of an earl – hence the name of his autobiography.

Ian Fleming, the famous author who himself spent a lot of time there, called Herbert "the Queen Mother of Tangier." And another writer said that in Tangier Herbert was no longer a younger son but "a minor potentate who decided who was socially acceptable" – and more important, who was not acceptable.

David Herbert on right, with Paul Bowles, Cecil Beaton & Jane Bowles

Herbert, for example, disapproved of another well-known expat, David Edge, whom he considered a fraud (there is more about both Davids in the final chapter, the Epilogue). Herbert would find out who had been to Edge's parties and make sure none of them were invited to Barbara Hutton's.

Barbara Hutton was of course the Woolworth's heiress who reigned, almost like a real queen, over the Tangier social events and who threw the most wonderful parties. She herself seems to have been very fond of the other sort of queen, perhaps because there was no emotional involvement.

16
Telling it all

First part by Adrian Hammond and then an interview with PeterKendall

Tangier's Grand Socco during the Iinternational Zone years, 1920-1957

Paul Bowles's autobiography "Without Stopping" was nicknamed "Without Telling" since it was so reticent on gay matters. I suppose we are really at the stage now, half a century later, of being able to give the <u>whole</u> story of gays going out to Tangier, without such a reticence. Now we can indeed tell it all.

The idea of gays going abroad into sunny climes to seek an Adonis had of course arisen in the nineteenth century. The favoured places had perhaps been Algiers and Tunis[10]. Then in the Edwardian era it had been southern Italy, especially Capri. Gradually came in the idea that less favoured or less rich people could go abroad too – in search of sea, sand, sunshine and perhaps a fourth thing too.

---

[10] Described in Chapter 2

It is true that both Paris and Berlin were humming with gay activity in the 1920s, with only occasional police raids, but there was still the lure of sunnier foreign climes by the sea. The Fascist takeover in Italy in 1922 almost coincided with the beginning of the International Zone in Tangier, so inevitably gays were now more drawn to Tangier, which promised freedom and safety, rather than to Italy with its new xenophobic government in Rome.

`This was not only because Tangier was an attractive, sunny seaside resort but it was also an international zone, where they could well feel safer than in many other places. There would be comforting things such as British, Spanish and French post offices, yet without either the restrictive European sexual laws or the feared rule of a foreign dictator.

Tangier: the Spanish post office (left) and the British one (right)

The phrases "live and let live" or "each to his own" became bywords for the lifestyle in the International Zone of Tangier, and from the 1920s it became a haven for those wanting more freedom than on offer in their own lands. Many of them were, unsurprisingly, homosexual, as in those days it was against the law in North America and all European countries (except in France up to 1940).

Tangier's Socco Chico c.1925, with a mix of classes/ races evident and with the awnings of the Café Central just visible lower right.

The Encyclopaedia of Homosexuality has a section entitled "Homosexual Questors". A short extract:: "The fact that travel and exploration generally involved being in the company of other men and requiring the company of friendly locals to act as guides and servants is bound to have a stronger appeal to homosexual than to heterosexual men....there long flourished a homosexual colony in Tangier, exotic but near to Europe."

Paul Bowles exemplified the whole Tangier experience, since he was gay (or bi-), intelligent, relaxed, sociable and with a desire for a new way of life which he felt the city could satisfy. Despite being mainly happily married to Jane, during the time that he was in Tangier Bowles formed several friendships with young men, who were usually his protégés. He would encourage them in their strivings as artists, for example Ahmed Yacoubi, or as writers, for example Mohammed Mrabet and Choukri. Both Bowles, husband and wife, were of a gay orientation and, although they had mutual toleration, their respective partners/protégés often took dislikes to each other. Jane had ambivalent but intense relationships with Moroccan women, and there could be tension between their Moroccan friends.

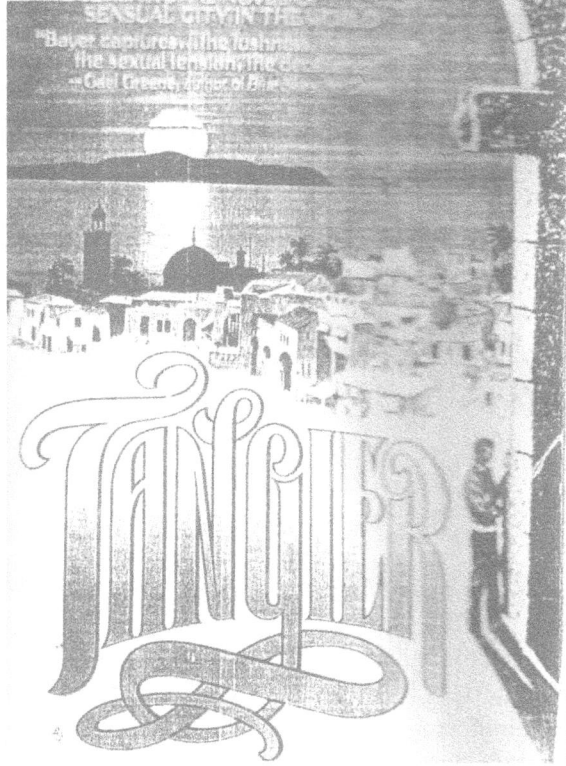

"Tangier," a novel by William Bayer, with   sub-title
"The most sensual city in the world".

There is a scene based on truth in the gripping novel "Tangier" by William Bayer, where all the English expats are invited to a big picnic on Tangier beach, on condition that each brings his young Moroccan friend along too. (Needless to say problems arise once they are all assembled there.) The scene may have been fictitious but there was a strong tradition in Tangier for many of the gentlemen keeping to the *same* Moroccan friend for some time and developing a long-term relationship. They had found, if you like, their Adonis and did not want to let him go.

Many of the expats sought such long-term and stable relationships with young male Moroccans, and the mutual benefits in such relationships were obvious. Examples of beneficial relationships were Paul Bowles with Choukri and Mrabet, as he translated their literary works for them. But there was also Genet with Katrani and Azzedine in Larache[11], and even Burroughs formed a long relationship with a Spaniard named Kiki, who was eighteen when they first met. With the Burroughs relationship, for example, both sides gained – Kiki receiving help for his sick mother and for his education and Burroughs being inspired, as he relates himself:

"When I am with Kiki I get ideas for writing faster and better than at other times…He is a sort of medium through which I get ideas."

Ron Nelson [12] who was known to many of us as a friend, was a case in hand. Over the years he formed several long-term relationships with young Moroccans, the relationships only coming to an end when the young man concerned wanted to get married around the age of twenty seven – this being almost compulsory for them in those days. He kept his job in South London but would go out at every available holiday to see them.

David Herbert also had a long-term gay relationship with James Caffery, a nephew of the American ambassador to Paris whom he met whilst visiting London. After Herbert had finally persuaded the young man to make his home with him in Tangier, Caffery decided unfortunately that he just did not like the expat community and preferred the Spanish one (which was large in those days), always choosing Spanish rather than Moroccan servants.

Eventually Caffery left Herbert and went off with a Spaniard, with whom he set up an antique shop in Spain. Herbert's explanation of why their relationship broke down is not without interest. He explained that he had volunteered to take part in a pantomime organised by the expats to raise money for charity:–

"The Spaniard, though admitting that my performance (as a panto dame) was good, said how ugly I looked. Jamie's affection for

---

[11] Chapter 40 is on Genet and Larache

[12] Ron Nelson's contributions are in Chapters 20 and 26

me seemed to wane from that moment. It was sad that our friendship was broken up after twelve years, but sadder still that the break was caused by my playing the part of a female in aid of charity."

Editor: Just for the record, Herbert had had some experience in the world of theatre when young, because during the late 1920s he had sung, played the piano and acted at a cabaret nightclub in Berlin. So here is now a photo of Herbert in pantomime drag, and readers will see how at home he was in costume:

Barbara Hutton and David Herbert in fancy dress

Editor continues: Over now to someone who knew Tangier way back in the 1950s. We are pleased now to include the first of our several interviews, a memoir from someone who went on holiday there in the 1950s, as it gives such a good flavour of the atmosphere then. The interview took place between Peter Kendall, who has sadly since passed away, Rowan Tudor and myself. It was set up very kindly by Rowan in 2005. So here is what we learned in the interview:–

Peter and his friend had arrived in Tangier in the early 1950s, at a time when you were only allowed to take fifty pounds out of the UK.

They of course got to know some of the other gentlemen in Tangier. For example there was Mr Brown, who had a sharp sense of humour and, similar to the slightly juvenile but amusing practice in Agadir, he set up the idea of giving nicknames, often of a female nature, to the gentlemen in Tangier. He would refer to one rather sarcastic gentleman as 'Vinegar Lil,' and to an American gay couple (one half of whom was rather vicious in nature – but the other half a harmless old dear) – as 'Arsenic and Old Lace.'

During their time in the Zone of course Peter and his friend formed meaningful relationships with some of the youths there, and had been only too happy to let them have some of their rather precious supply of money. The lads hanging out around the port area had been exceptionally friendly and charming.

Then they decided to hire a car and go exploring the east of the country on their own. Unfortunately, however, they accidentally strayed out of the Spanish zone and into the French controlled area. The French officials, who were dealing with an insurrection against their colonial rule, considered them to be spies and would not believe a word of their story, refusing also to accept their "carnet" – the system of identity papers then in operation.

Eventually they allowed them to go, but gave them a very hefty fine indeed (it was probably a racket), with the result that they arrived back in Tangier, not just with their tails between their legs but completely and totally broke!

Around the port they met the same small group of lads again, who of course asked for a little more money. On being told that their English friends were both penniless and homeless, the lads became genuinely kind and concerned. They found, for the two Englishmen, some empty packing containers on the port side which they made into two little homes for them with bedding and simple furniture.

In addition to this, they brought them fresh fish for which they had dived, caught and then cooked, plus bread taken from their own homes. The whole thing was apparently completely charming and idyllic, and when they finally got some money sent to them they were sad when it all came to an end. The two young Moroccans proved that, if they were ever given a chance to repay kindnesses they'd received themselves, they would gladly take it.

End of interview

A short quote from Jane Bowles' diary, 1948:
"The Tangier of that January night was a place of mystery, a city of arches. Veiled women in white robes and men in hoods and cloaks moved silently through the by-streets. The trees everywhere were filled with birds. As I walked alone, I came across wooden packing crates in the streets. Lights flickered inside them. I peeped in and saw people cooking and eating and sleeping."

Tangier between the wars

The kindness of Tanjawis

The phrase "I have always depended on the kindness of strangers" was penned by another gay Tangerino, Tennessee Williams. Kindness certainly came into Peter's story above about the packing case homes, and it's interesting that both Peter Kendall in this chapter and also Peter Lever back in Chapter Four mention the kindness and often good-naturedness of the Tangier lads.

Perhaps I could briefly mention something on "the interview which never took place". It should have been with Dennis Callan, who visited Tangier several times in the 1960s and 1970s. Having taken a religious vow and living abroad, however, he decided not to contribute to this book, but he wishes us well (as we do him).

He did tell me, however, that one memory above all others remains with him from Tangier. A young friend, with whom he had been involved, met him by chance on the hill near the Muniria, and quite spontaneously gave him a long and affectionate hug, yet wanting nothing in return. End of story.

So if you put the comments of the two Peters and of Dennis together, perhaps the reputation of Tangier youth for being hard and uncaring was not always justified.

Tangier, with Grand Socco in foreground and Spain in far distance

17
Café Society in Tangier

Our second and third (separate) interviews were with Horace Gendell and Rowan Tudor. The theme of café society came into both of them.

The aptly named BBC Café, a regular meeting place for expats

Horace begins: The beach cafés were, for almost everyone, favourite places to meet. One of them was the BBC Café [13]. It had been run by one of the great expat characters of Tangier named Emma Bodenz, referred to as "mine hoste par excellence". BBC actually stood for "Beach Bar Carousel" but the appeal of the name was obvious.

Another famous landmark for the gentlemen was of course the Windmill Café, which later became one of Joe Orton's favourite places. In those days the beach was divided into two by a fence – one half ostensibly for the Moroccans and one for the Europeans. The Windmill was conveniently between the two sections.

Equally convenient there was a changing room under the café ostensibly for swimmers – you could tell the chappie on the

[13] It was frequented by several friends described in this book, such as Ralph Burton and Ron Nelson.

door that you had a friend coming in there and there would never be any problems. The café was run by two English guys and they kept a good supply of Earl Grey tea, scones and Cornish pasties for us.

A quick digression to tell you about the hammam (baths) near the Petit Socco which was also great fun in those days. It was run by a friendly local gentleman, and one went in, discreetly followed by one's friend some paces behind, and paid for two.

One was then led to a number of olive green coloured doors. You found yourself in a small ante-room with a wooden bench along one wall and some hooks on the wall above with wooden hangers. Bolting the door behind you, you then undressed and put your clothes on the hangers or bench. Then another door would open and one's chosen young companion would come in and bolt that one too!

Paddling across the tiles he joined you in the ante-room, took off his clothes and then both stepped into a slightly sunken and totally tiled adjacent room. The companion put the plug in, turned on the huge taps sticking out, until the hot water started. Usually one waited until the water would be up to a foot deep, then standing in this mini-pool you soaped and cleaned each other, then lay in the hot water and enjoyed a massage, a cuddle, or wallowed around in joy...

Back to cafés and bars after that digression! In the centre of town, Dean's Bar could often be interesting if you wanted a drink in the evening, although I never saw the boy dancers whom Maugham described. In fact there were several other livelier bars, such as Scott's, which I sometimes visited.

The Parade Bar was also very good to meet English friends, but in the 1960s I recall that those gentlemen who liked the somewhat older young Moroccans headed off towards Scotts Bar, behind the Rue Pasteur, whilst those who liked the somewhat younger ones usually found what they were looking for around the Petit Socco – they were often just standing around waiting for them.

A couple named Tom and Jeremy, one of whom was of Chinese origin, had a large place on the "Mountain" and a restaurant in Gibraltar. (By the way, expats who lived in Tangier would often hop on the Mons Calpe ferry and chug over to Gib for lunch, and probably go to the bank, post letters, etc.)

Wintry views of the Windmill Café on Tangier beach
(made famous by Joe Orton), a year before demolition

I also remember that quite often expats met for tea and sticky buns at the Windmill, or at another Brit-run beach café called, I think, "Adonis" which had a picture of a well-muscled be-speedo'd young man on the door to the beach level changing room area. I think that the Adonis was for the more "butch crowd" than the Windmill.

They were a lovely couple of gays who ran the Adonis, I remember, always laughing and talking to you in that way gays used to in the 1960s : "Ooo, get you dear, in your new hat! ...Here, come and have a vada who's chasing who on the beach...Ooo, how bold!... There – he's got him."

Now Rowan Tudor: I think people over-emphasise the importance of the Windmill because it was written about by Joe Orton. My experience was that the title of the "best beach café in town" was often changing. Before the Windmill, for example, it had been the Sun Beach (the only one owned by a Brit, James Duncan, and the farourite one of Tennessee Williams, who wrote part of "Cat On a Hot Tin Roof" there). Then a few years later it would be the BBC beach café, and so on.

There were a number of reasons for this – just changing fashion or maybe one café being a bit too bold and brazen, thus producing a small clampdown, usually by the management.

The other thing I wanted to mention was that the lads who worked in these cafés were often friendly and looking for European friends. One of their jobs in the beach cafés was to look after the clothes of the Europeans because you were not allowed on a certain section of the beach except in swim gear – their way of keeping the locals away. They were sort of friendly young Moroccans acting as gentle "beach police" making sure everything was okay.

The Tanger Inn was often interesting although they only seemed to have one record playing there ("Brown girl in the ring, tra la la la la") which could slightly drive you mad. Those who were most friendly with the proprietors John and Peter were allowed to take their young friends there for a drink, with discretion. A guy called Bryn brought good looking youths over from England – a case of coals to Newcastle if ever there was one! – and used to drink with them in the Tanger Inn. I think he may have used them as bait to attract the younger, good looking Moroccans.

I enjoyed Scott's Bar rather a lot – it had been started by an Englishman named John Scott and survived a lot longer than most other places. (I used to like the murals which were painted by Stuart Church and depicted Moroccan boys in kilts.) You could meet all sorts of people in Scotts. A friend of mine named Joe was one evening asked to dance by a man whom he was sure he knew but he just could *not* think where he'd met him before... He eventually worked out it was his daughter's headmaster, and he had last spoken to him at a parents' evening!

That very last story is a reminder that Tangier was perhaps one of the few places in those days to which many professional-class gays, like that schoolmaster, could safely go to "be themselves".

Now Paul Horler will tell us now about two other famous cafés:

Porte's Salon de Thé on the corner of Rue de Goya, as it was recently

Madame Porte, said to be of Swiss origin, opened a *salon de thé* catering for the French, in the Socco Chico in the early 1930s. She became disliked in the war, however, as she was suspected of being a Nazi sympathiser and her café was said to be a centre of espionage. Madame Porte herself was never in any case sociable, either during or after the war, and rarely left her place behind the cash desk.

The tearoom and bakery functioned for many years and was said to do the best cakes and cocktails in all Morocco, being full of slightly upmarket Europeans during the later years of the International Zone. It relocated twice, once in 1951 to the Rue du Statut and then a couple of years later to its present site. The third venue was/is stylish with marble floors and art deco mouldings.

Madame Porte's salon de thé became a place of refuge for those expats growing perhaps tired of the downmarket and grasping side of Tangier life. Jane Bowles used to take Tennessee Williams in there when, during the very bad winter of 1948, he had started to grow tired of the city and needed some encouragement to stay. (Paul Bowles was writing the score for some of Tennessee's plays).

During the years of struggle for independence the nationalist leader, Torres, frequented it – he could not be arrested in the international zone. It also became a popular centre for socialisation, being highly regarded by the elegant ladies in the European community (probably of both genders!) who would take coffee there at eleven. It was also popular with the likes of raffish Australian George Greaves who would hold court there every evening between 6 and 7, since alcohol was also served. Alec Waugh[14] was another regular there in the 1960s – wearing his white suits and large broad-brimmed white hat, he would go there every evening for an extra-large cocktail.

By the 1970s, of course, the Portes had long since passed away, and bourgeois Moroccans had replaced the sadly dwindling numbers in the European community as the main customers.

Let's not forget the importance of the Café de Paris either, [15] located at one end of the Boulvard Pasteur and opposite the French Consulate. In the late 60s and 70s, towards the end of the "golden years", it became a favourite meeting place, being mentioned in the Orton diaries: Joe Orton suggested to some straight tourists on the tables outside the café that they should move on, as they had "no right to be occupying chairs reserved for decent sex perverts."

It's worth remembering that members of Tangier's high society such as David Herbert rarely went to the Socco Chico, and in fact by the 1960s the Café Central was beginning to be considered down-market even by the middle-of-the-roaders. So people like Orton, Halliwell and Tennessee Williams started to find the Café de Paris, situated just away from the Medina, perhaps more congenial and sympathetic.

---

[14] one of the writers described in Chapter 15

[15] A photo of Cafe de Paris on p. 81, and stories about it on p. 160 and p.183

18
Friendships between the races

Reminiscences by Peter Robins, Horace Gendell and Rowan Tudor: this chapter is about friendships between Tanjawis (the native inhabitants) and Tangerinos (the gay expat resident/ holiday-makers).

Peter Robins starts:
I had not intended to do more than pass through Morocco – well, Tangier to be exact – on my way to holiday with my friends who were working just beyond the Algerian border in Oran. It was 1971. We were all a lot younger and a bit more adventurous in those days. Well, those unencumbered by families I mean. I'd spotted an advertisement in one of our weekend papers for a new ferry service from Southampton to Tangier via Lisbon.

Seizing on the chance of a three day wind-down after a hectic year in London, I made my booking. I also contacted a couple of friends I knew who returned year after year to an apartment they had booked in Tangier. They cabled by return that they had reserved a room for one night at the hotel which I came to know as the Tanger Inn but was also called the Muniria.

The journey through the Bay of Biscay, the bus tour of Lisbon and the company on my outward journey provided the therapy I had anticipated. At the quayside in Tangier Mike and John welcomed me. A brief taxi ride and they steered me to the hotel reception.

Having left me to unpack they returned an hour later – and off we went to the Petit Socco. Settling down with my back to the open window of the Café Central I was waiting for a tea with citron when Mike broke the news to me: an outward journey by train to Algeria would be nowhere like as easy as I had supposed.

What was to be done? Very thoughtfully Mike had had a further 14 days pencilled in at the hotel. It was as I considered this that John interjected with "Look over there. It's that actor from television!"

I did look and, as I lit my cigarette, felt a tap on my shoulder. A young Moroccan was looking through the full-length open window behind me indicating he too would like a light. I obliged and, in doing so, held his gaze until we both found ourselves smiling.

That is how I met Omar – with whom I shared meals, trips of exploration, and visits to his father's extensive farm some ten miles out of the city.

Once we were known and trusted at one of the little restaurants away from the tourist beat, we were served "special" lemonade or a very acceptable local red wine in a well-washed coca cola bottle.

I see I haven't mentioned the afternoons. Well, that was siesta time wasn't it? After all, my bedroom looked out onto the Mediterranean. Omar and I shared everything else, so why not the double divan?

Tangier harbour, c.1950. On the left of the jetty
is the Atlantic, on the right the Mediterranean

Rowan Tudor continues:
In the late 1960s many Europeans wanted to find a flat – usually situated in the Ville Nouvelle end of the town, rather than in the Medina. The problem about the Medina was that the women were always up on the roof putting their washing out and they acted as sentinels to report on anything untoward (for instance a visiting European) which might be happening.

Horace continues:

An Englishman who had a very appropriate name like Mr. Lockwood had many flats on offer in the Ville Nouvelle. Concierges in flats hardly ever had any problems about you bringing back youths or young men. Of course you showed your appreciation, but it was never asked for in a threatening way.

Around the same time, a stooped German ran a TV repair shop (located in a little alley just downhill from the Socco Chico and Cafe Central) where he would be training up a few young apprentices, all of whom were delighted to be given such a chance. Heinrich had a fascination for young things who were attached to big things, if you see what I mean, and they were often his apprentices – it was actually a really good start for them in life.

There were so many expat English at the time in Tangier, I recall, and often they would be "the black sheep of the family", having got into trouble of various kinds, not always homosexual, and having been sent out to Tangier to keep them out of the way.

I shared a flat in Tangier with two American friends. We had a pair of young Moroccan friends whom I specially remember. Abdul liked prancing naked around the flat – although he always kept a gold chain round his waist. (I expect he'd been told it was wrong to have nothing on.)

He was always smiling but he annoyed the other youth, Mohamed, since he was so untidy and – completely unforgiveable – he was always dropping crumbs over the floor. Mohamed on the other hand fussed all day to keep everything spick 'n' span.

Mohamed was also very proud to do the shopping (either in the shops or in the Grand Socco) – indeed begged to do it since it showed that we trusted him with the money. Returning with the right food and the right change was a huge boost to his confidence.

The local shop keepers treated him as a person of real substance because he brought trade to their door. I am sure he played on this as he would bring back treats for himself and Abdul, which were not from out of our money, and were probably given to him as a tip by shop/stall keepers.

The Grand Socco in the early1960s, with much buying and selling

If there was a lot to carry, Mohammed would bully Abdul, who was a larger and tougher character, into riding shotgun as protection and to carry the heavier bags. I don't think either of them was ever exhausted (although in a certain respect they knew how to exhaust their hosts!) since they were very appreciative of having clean beds to sleep in and as much food as they liked. In fact Mr Lockwood recommended them to others as house servants because they were utterly honest, very clean, worked hard and were just huge fun to have around. So we enjoyed their company over quite a number of years.

Mohammed would have quite a tiring day of housework – cooking, washing up, scrubbing the floor and shopping. So at the end of the day the young house-husband would flop down into our double bed, sighing deeply and saying: 'Ahhh – at *last* we can have some fun!'

Days out of town, either in the company of friends or not, were another great source of joy. As you travelled along the road shepherd lads, some just wearing a thobe (Arabic robe) with nothing under it, would wave your car down and would be very happy to present their credentials.

Now over to Rowan again:

During the 1960s I had taken an apartment in Tangier, near to the fishmarket. The market made it very noisy early in the morning but it didn't worry me too much as I was up on the roof and had a wonderful view of what was going on. The apartment was like a hutch stuck on top of the flat roof.

One of the first people I got to know was the agent who found me the flat. I remember him saying to me "Vous devez vivre bourgeoisment. Pas de vas-et-vients constamment." (One can guess from that, the kind of problems he had been having with other European tenants!).

The tenant below me was named Absalem and he was the former boy-friend of a quite famous academic in England who was considered then an expert on homosexuality. Absalem gave me quite a bit of advice on the Tangier scene, some of it more useful than the rest. On one occasion I just could not get rid of a really ugly and pushy tout who followed me round wherever I went. So I told Absalem my problem and he said he would find me someone *really* nice, the lad of my dreams.

Thus I was quite excited later that day when Absalem knocked on the hutch door with a big smile and said "Here, dream boy!" He pushed the young Moroccan forward. Who was it? – yes, the same tout I couldn't get rid of!

More worrying, by this time the academic had found a new and younger boyfriend, and Absalem was threatening to spoil the new one's looks by pushing a broken bottle into his face. I think it was then that I decided to leave Tangier for a while.

However, I came back a couple of years later and met Absalem again. He had got married and seemed a lot calmer now – or he did at first! Unfortunately I met his friend named Mohamed who asked me for a little financial help, which I gave. But when Absalem found out I had given him money he flew into another rage and accused my of having an affair with Mohamed, which as it happens I wasn't. Absalem went on getting angrier and angrier about my supposed affair with Mohamed.

Now round about that time there was a lot in the news about lie-detectors and so I volunteered to go over to Gibraltar and have one done. I think he then believed me!

There were a lot of servants who would be youngish or oldish lads, and if one of the Europeans was holding a party he would say "Could I borrow your Saleem for my party?" . The boys much enjoyed going to another house since they would be well paid for special occasions and it was the chance to meet new people. In about 1986, for example, we held a "Festschrift" for Paul Bowles to celebrate the launching of his latest book, and on that occasion a lot of houseboys were pooled as servants.

I remember a friend called Joe had a cleaning boy who had married but went on cleaning for him over a number of years. Eventually Joe introduced him to a friend called Hugh who specialised in television aerials and he was taken on by Hugh to be trained as a technician because Joe had recommended him so highly. So his nickname changed from 'Cleaning Boy Ahmed' to 'Aerial Ahmed'!

Another expat named Eric, who was German, ran a hamburger café and he employed several lads who were dressed in smart sailor uniforms and looked very fetching indeed in their caps. So all in all I think a lot of the lads did very well through us being there and they got many chances to learn a trade. (One Englishman even bought his young friend a taxi as a business.)

Another example. Budd was an American who came regularly every year and stayed for just ten weeks. During that time his houseboy Absalem always appeared and was completely faithful to him. During the other forty two weeks of the year, however, he was available for others as a houseboy (I mean servant), but he was always devoted to Budd for those ten weeks.

Of course the friendships and the flirtation went on at the same time. I think my main friend amongst the English was Mr Brown, whom Peter Kendall mentioned in his interview with you. On one occasion I took a photo of a stunningly beautiful young Moroccan I had seen around. I showed the photo to Mr Brown and he burst out laughing!

"Come on back to my flat," he said quietly.

When we got there I found he had locked a houseboy into his flat – and who should it be but the beauty in the photo!

Now the phrase "locked a houseboy into his flat" probably sounds very sinister, but it really wasn't. An expat might leave one locked in the flat while he went out for a coffee etc. The young

Moroccan would have as much food as he wanted, could watch the television and whatever. But the door had to be locked or else he might, for instance, disappear with all the valuables, or he might invite all his friends round for a party. It was an arrangement which they understood and were quite happy about. They were free to leave, if they wanted to, as soon as we returned.

It's worth remembering, by the way, that a lot of the older Moroccans were having their own fun and games – they had their own "scene", carrying on and making friends with lads in their own way, with their own jealousies and on their own terms. You would sort of gather it was going on, but of course never told the details.

Moving on to other expat characters now. Nigel was another acquaintance of mine amongst the Tangerinos and I think he is mentioned in the Orton diaries. He was friends with the artist Francis Bacon, who lived in the town. After Francis had passed away Nigel found many of his hitherto unknown paintings in his flat. (Nigel was related to the founders of a famous biscuit firm back in the UK. He was always waiting to inherit a fortune – he did finally inherit it but then very sadly died a short time later, so never really got the benefit.)

Another friend was called Tom Linton from South Africa; he actually set up an apartment within his house for his former houseboy, who by this time was married with children. He became a sort of grandfather figure to the children. Tom's nickname was Bella and the joke amongst the other expats was that he would never get round to actually doing anything with any of the young (unmarried) men who were obviously available. He thought that any of them who *were* available would automatically be loose-living and not pure enough for him!

One of the expats made up a series of poems about the various characters in Tangier, and here is part of the one about Bella:

> Looking for lands of licence, one year in early Feb,
> She found a pied-a-terre, in the kingdom of Maghreb.
> Ever the hungry hunter, our Bella never rested,
> And every time she met a youth his willingness she tested.
> The chatting up that now went on was not to be believed,
> But all their hopes were falsely raised and soon to be deceived.

The splendid youth, who oft implored, comes knocking at the door
Is by that very act confirmed, as "just another whore."
Alone at home sits Bella, her virgo still intact,
Awash it seems, in sexual dreams, though still afraid to act.
The words "Nil desperandum" are written on her door,
And, with luck, a Mister Right is due to call at four.

A final word from Horace:

All of these lads were completely guilt-free and had none of the inhibitions one would associate with western youths. Nobody told them they were being taken advantage of, and I don't believe the thought ever entered their head.

For them, having a friendship with a western man was a huge bonus, an opportunity very often to better themselves and a source of joy and pride amongst their own friends.

19
Four Famous Journalists
by Adrian Hammond

There were four expatriate and journalistic names who set about making Morocco, and Tangier in particular, known to the public back home.

The first and the earliest of these was **Walter Harris**, the Times correspondent, who wrote a number of travel books increasing knowledge of the country in the early twentieth century.

Walter Harris

His own private life was said to be eccentric. Having just married a titled Englishwoman, to prove herself worthy of him he forced her to ride on horseback through a river to the villa – which Walter had just had built on the eastern seashore of Tangier (Villa Harris).

She succeeded in this with flying colours, but her first night with Walter did not go so smoothly. Still fired with boldness, the brave lass decided to do something even more bold – to enter her lord and master's room even though she had been told not to. Guess what? Yes, as she entered in the early hours she found him in bed with a young male Moroccan! So distressed was she by the experience that she spent the rest of the night on top of the wardrobe and refused to come down. Next day she took refuge in the British legation and never returned to her husband.

Or so they say... The lady's relatives gave a different version of the story, saying she had fled from the house because Walter was so occupied with creating the garden for his house that she felt she would die of boredom. (Mind you, the break-up could have been a combination of *both* factors.)

He was a wonderful raconteur when he met people in the Socco Chico at the Café Central, and was said to be the only person who could tell the same story twelve times but with enough variation each time to make it interesting each time. His book "The Morocco That Was" is still very good reading.

But we must end this section a bit more seriously. Walter was held in great respect by local people and he was involved in charitable work as well as serious journalism. Some years before, he had written "If a strong check were given to the liquor traffic and if the Christians would learn that Moors are men and not beasts, then and only then might we have some reason for expending philanthropy."

The inscription on his tombstone reads: "He loved the Moorish people and was their friend."[16]

Rom Landau is the second of the four Tangier journalistic expats. In his book "Moroccan Journal" published in 1952 and relating to his journeys in the 1940s, he has quite a lot to say about the subject of homosexuality, vis-a-vis young Moroccans, which makes unusual reading. It has a patronising colonial tone to it, but is certainly not without interest. On the next page is an extract. (He uses the word "Moor" for Moroccan which seems to have disappeared soon after.):

---

[16] On page 177 readers can see a picture of his funeral at St Andrews in 1933, where both Christians and Muslims have gathered to pay their last respects to him.

"Throughout the Muslim world sexual practice is but lightly affected by the moral implications which are accepted in the Christian concept. For the average Moor the sexual act is one of the natural manifestations, and as such differs little in importance from the appeasement of thirst and hunger...there are few of the conscious or automatic responses which to some extent control the sex life of European peoples. To this relative lack of restraint we must add the extraordinary virility of the Moors... for a people bereft of worldly riches and imbued with a potent virility and recognising few moral restraints, sexual gratification is the chief enjoyment .

"Several schoolmasters, both French and native, have told me that one of the chief handicaps of the Moorish boy is his sexual precocity.... As soon as sexual awareness takes possession, it almost invariably assumes a disproportionate significance in their lives, and in their anxiety to give it full rein they let their studies go by default......Without necessarily being homosexual he will often indulge in homo-erotic practices... Such practices are encouraged by the strict segregation of the sexes... "

Michael Davidson was the third of the famous journalists who wrote about his times in Morocco. His second book "Some Boys" concentrated on his personal gay exploits with younger males in various countries, but his first book "The World, the Flesh and Myself" told more about his work as a journalist.

In one section of "The World..." he describes the political situation in Morocco in 1947. The French had been cultivating the Sultan Mohamed as a kind of puppet ruler in Morocco and they thought that by paying him a lot of money they could keep him sweet and compliant. Davidson was a witness when the sultan met the French governor-general. The latter found that the sultan was anything *but* compliant. In the middle of polite conversation, the sultan (who would eventually become Moroccan king Mohamed V) suddenly interrupted and said "I hope General, that you have come to do justice to Moroccan aspirations?"

Davidson reported on all this. But even more dramatic, Davidson found out that the Sultan was planning to take a train from Rabat to Tangier where he would proclaim the Moroccan wish for independence from France, Tangier being the safest place for him to do it since it was under international control.

He now tells the tale in his own words:

"No breath of it had yet leaked out; I had the story to myself. The enormous importance to North Africa's future seemed obvious...I had, I knew, a world scoop. I went to Tangier on board the royal train (the only European), with the Shereefian flags about its engine. A triumph in Rome must have looked like a village fete beside that imperial progress!

An artist's impression of Davidson

"The single track railway was lined by delighted Moors... Then Tangier, crammed with tribesmen from mountain and plain, was as turbulently joyful as London on VE night...

"Good old George Greaves met me at Tangier station and put me up during the royal stay; and more important took me to Dean's Bar and to Dean himself – it was like being presented to a cardinal; and therafter I wondered how the Tangier I'd known six years before could have existed without Dean and his Bar."

Davidson was thus able to report the whole story of the sultan's dramatic train journey to the outside world. A scoop indeed.

Rupert Croft-Cooke was the fourth journalist who brought a knowledge of Morocco to Europe. In the 1950s and later he wrote a whole series of books about his experiences in Morocco, very different in tone to that of Rom Landau and Michael Davidson. The three main books covering his time in Tangier are "The Tangerine House", "The Exiles" and "The Caves of Hercules." The latter he describes as being "an account, candid to the limit of good manners, of the later period of my fourteen years' residence in Tangier, and finally shows why I decided to leave it!"

"In the Parade Bar, Tangier," wrote Croft-Cooke, "I met as many people of repute as I did in Bar la Mar Chica, from the Dame of Sark to Cecil Beaton, from Helena Bernstein to Ian Fleming."

RUPERT CROFT-COOKE

Croft-Cooke was not as "upper class" as some of the other residents there and he probably suffered from a feeling of inferiority, never quite fitting into either the upper class parties or, at the other end of the spectrum, into the very relaxed goings-on in Dutch Tony's and the Socco Chico. The various autobiographies he wrote about his life in Tangier, especially "The Caves of Hercules", were probably his way of settling scores with other Tangerinos.

One person Croft-Cooke did get on well with, however, was Noel Coward – who made occasional trips out to Tangier, as well as other parts of Morocco such as Mazagan/el Jadida. Coward probably found that the *intensity* of some of the love affairs between Tangerinos and Tanjawis reminded him just a little of the straight ones featured in his own plays like "Hay Fever" and in his own songs like "Mad about the boy".

Cooke discovered Noel one day in Dean's Bar reading one of his (Cooke's) books, and a conversation was struck up between them.

Cooke commented to Coward, during their short holiday friendship, that if they had met ten years previously they would probably have been social rivals and would have hated each other.

"Whereas," replied Coward, with his usual clipped vowels, "twenty years ago, it would have been an affair."

Illustrating, perhaps, the three ages of Gay Man?

Noel Coward

Michael Davidson, as you will have read above, had broken the news about one of the most famous events in Tangier's history, namely the arrival of the Sultan and the declaring of independence for Morocco. But Croft-Cooke was able to break the news of one of the most *infamous,* namely the Great Scandal of 1958.

The separate status of Tangier had ended with Moroccan independence in 1957, and only a year later the expats were caught up in this scandal, which made them think that the Paradise for gays in their city was coming to a sudden and dramatic end.

Croft-Cooke described how it happened. The first thing that sparked off the purge was the disappearance of a 15 year old Spanish boy in Tangier whose parents reported the matter to the police. It turned out that he had run away for a lark and, not so unusual for Spanish youths, was earning pocket money amongst the Europeans. But he was alive, happy and well.

The second thing that set the purge in action, surprisingly, slightly involved that most respectable of all the gay expats, Paul Bowles. One of his protégés, Ahmed Yacoubi was charged with having sex with a German teenager on holiday there. In the aftermath of these two events a fair number of arrests were made, and several well-known expats, such as Dutch Tony (described in next chapter) left Tangier and went to Gibraltar.

The purge ended after a few weeks. David Woolman, who tended to be a fountain of all knowledge in old Tangier, felt that it was the intervention of King Hassan II which stopped the purge, as he did not want the country to become anti-foreigner.

Life returned to more or less "normal", as proved by the fact that Joe Orton thoroughly enjoyed himself with the younger locals some nine years later. But it was perhaps a warning to the expats that things would one day completely change, and that the special laissez-faire atmosphere of Tangier would eventually come to an end.

Croft-Cooke in any case decided to leave Tangier in 1968, having decided it had changed for the worse. He was probably wise in this decision as, not long after in 1972, another scandal hit Tangier when an attempt was made on the king's life there. There followed another very general clampdown by the authorities, and it was round about that time Agadir started to become the favoured place for the European gentlemen to visit or to live.

20
Petit Socco and Café Central
compiled by the Editor

Tangier's Petit Socco and Café Central in about 1910

Called in French the Petit Socco and in Spanish the Socco Chico, this was the centre of ordinary Tangier life for many decades. Although the clothes of the people changed over the years a great deal from those in the above photo, the buildings hardly altered from 1910 to 1980. Its focal point during all those years was the Café Central.

The first mention of the Café Central was when it was a bar in late Victorian times, run by a Cypriot named Antonio. He had a piano on which customers were free to play all the tunes from London, Paris, Berlin or Rome, so perhaps it was already becoming an international meeting place. Walter Harris was of course there, but there were other eminent people such as the French novelist Pierre Loti and the conductor of the Munich opera's orchestra, Herr Levy.

In the 1920s you could still meet Walter Harris, plus his later friends – Richard Hughes (author of the classic "High Wind to Jamaica"), the painter James Wyllie and the polo player Jack Sinclair. As mentioned in an earlier chapter, evidence for André Gide having visited Tangier is not conclusive, but one of the tables in the Café Central was said in the past to have been always reserved for him.

In the 1950s? Well, Paul and Jane Bowles would have been in the café, as well as Djuna Barnes, the writer of the lesbian and decadence classic, "Nightwood", published 1936. She lived with her friend Charles Ford in a house which Bowles had found for them. Often Djuna would be seen at the Café Central with Bowles and Ford, she being the centre of attention with her face made up with blue, green and purple!

The author of the book "The Jews of Tangier" named Carlos Nesri was another regular customer. He used to ask the other European customers to sign his petition suggesting he should be awarded the Nobel Prize for literature.

More famous than Nesri, but also not awarded the Nobel Prize, was William Burroughs. In the mornings Burroughs would hold court at the Café, surrounded by his followers trying to get words of wisdom from the great man to record for posterity.

Burroughs also spent a lot of his time near the Café Central at Dutch Tony's which, as it was so close, we'll now digress to tell you about.

Dutch Tony's (right) in the Tangier Medina (Photo by Paul Horler)

Rather like the Tiggy later on in Agadir, Dutch Tony's was half boarding house and half male bordello. Tony Reithorst had arrived in Tangier just before the war, running his boarding house there until 1958 and, according to Woolman, he could arrange almost anything a client wanted. A liaison could also be started at the Café Central in the Socco Chico and then developed nearby at Dutch Tony's. (In the same way as a friendship between the races could, 25 years later in Agadir, be started at Café Navarros and then developed round the corner at the Tiggy!) When things got too busy at Dutch Tony's, with only a few bedrooms, the kitchen was used as a waiting room – either for those wanting services or for those offering.

Ginsberg and Burroughs in Dutch Tony's

In addition to Ginsberg and Burroughs (the latter stayed there two years before moving to the Muniria) famous guests, either staying or just visiting, included Robin Maugham, Tennessee Williams, Jack Kerouac, David Woolman himself and a fair number of others. Tony was liked by all who stayed there. He was said to dress in smart suits, wear makeup and walk his five poodles regularly, so maybe keeping a low profile wasn't his highest priority.

During the years of independence struggles, however, he became unpopular with locals and, as mentioned at the end of the last chapter, eventually he had to leave the city in 1958 during the short-lived but unpleasant police purge of that year.

Back now to William Burroughs in the Socco Chico itself: he had persuaded his friends Allen Ginsberg and Jack Kerouac to join him in Tangier, and these three – the most famous figures of the Beat generation – would often be seen together in the Café Central discussing drugs, sexual freedom and Zen Buddhism.

Rupert Croft-Cooke was friendly to the Beats when he met them but was scathing with his remarks about them in private, commenting that Burroughs wore suits sent by American charities to help poor Moroccans, and he couldn't even afford a typewriter.

Mind you, Croft-Cooke was by no means always too popular himself: David Woolman recorded that "he won a degree of admiration by continuing to sit at the Café Central smoking after he had just been hit on the head so hard by an irate Tanjawi newspaper boy that the heavy glass ash-tray used as a weapon was broken."

But there was the other end of the spectrum too. One of Paul Bowles' main protégés, Mohamed Choukri, described the sad kind of social apartheid that occurred in the old city in those days (the 40s and 50s): "All I knew of Tangier was the old city and the Petit Socco. I couldn't even go up to the Boulevard Pasteur."

Brian Howard was a less well-known writer than those described above, but his words written as he sat in the Café Central are worth recording: "I am in a café in the wickedest town in the world, and in the wickedest place in that town. .. ...I am in the Socco Chico where the naughtiest and most shameless male whores – not all Arab – show off their various wares."

Our last character in this chapter on the Café Central is Ron Nelson, whom we mentioned back in Chapter 16, and known to several contributors. (Our opening on the Café Central mentioned music being played there, and this closing story does too).

One afternoon, Ron and some of the gentlemen were drinking tea in the Central, listening to a rather camp musical quartet playing 'Palm Court Hotel' type of music on the roof of a shop next to the old Spanish post office. Sipping his tea, Ron plucked up courage and announced to his friends that, on his next Moroccan holiday, he would be staying in Marrakech rather than Tangier.

One of them looked at him wistfully and replied, "Oh, my dear friend, this means that we'll never see you here again!"

"Nonsense,." he said. "I'm just going to have a look round."

"Yes, but nobody ever comes back, once they've travelled further south," said his friend at the table.

Socco Chicco & Café Central, c.1940 [17]

In fact Ron Nelson never did return to Tangier, but it was Essaouira, not Marrakech, which became his favourite place. A few of Ron's anecdotes about Tangier and Essaouira were given to me by him while he was in hospital, in the few weeks before he passed away. [18]

---

[17] There is another view of the Socco Chico from opposite direction on page 89.

[18] Ron Nelson has another Tangier story in Chapter 26. His stories about Essaouira will hopefully be a part of our next volume on South Morocco "Agadir to My Heart.".

21
Five famous bars of old Tangier
by our resident historian, Paul Horler

Editor's introduction:
Some readers might well ask if these five famous bars, which Paul
will describe to you, were gay or not.

One could say that old Tangier, including the bars described,
had an ambience where society was not divided into straight and gay
and where the attitude "live and let live" was the norm. In that sense
the bars were, as they say nowadays, gay friendly. And do remember,
dear reader, that they existed at a time (the 1920s through to the
1960s) when the world outside was often anything *but* gay friendly; in
the UK, as you know, homosexuality was illegal until 1967, with the
age of consent for gays remaining 21 until after 1990 – and in other
countries close to Tangier things changed even more slowly.

The laws in the Tangier International Zone were often vague,
but there is general agreement that gays were freer there than
elsewhere. Lots of expats, quite a few of them British and gay, had
settled there and frequented these bars partly in order to meet
sympathetic people similar to themselves and seeking the same
freedoms. Upmarket places like "1001" and the Parade were often
for meeting other expat friends, and less affluent Moroccans would
have been discouraged from entering them (by the prices if nothing
else) unless they were actually with a foreign friend.

On the other hand, several of the bars, for example "Dean's"
and Bar la Mar Chica (the more downmarket ones), were known to
be relaxed places for gay friendship between the races to start.

Now over to Paul and the five famous bars:
Dean's Bar

In the 1930s the smart new British-owned Minzah hotel in the Rue
du Statut (now Rue de la Liberté) had a head barman called Joseph
Dean. He was a dapper well-spoken black man who, by his own very
changeable accounts, sprang from either Egyptian or West Indian
roots, had been educated at Westminster School or had been brought
up in France. Take your pick!

Dean left the Minzah under something of a cloud and opened his own bar just down the hill at 2 Rue Amerique du Sud, and this became "Dean's Bar". A small wall plaque put up in the 1990s says '1937'. The bar was described as unostentatious.

Deans's Bar in Tangier – first door on the left

Dean's Bar quickly became a popular meeting place for the international *glitterati*. Visitors included Cecil Beaton, Ian "triple vodka and tonic" Fleming and Cyril Connolly. The journalist Michael Davidson met author Robin Maugham there in the autumn of 1947. (Maugham was convinced, by the way, that Dean was a former crook, gigolo and Soho society drugs dealer named Donald Kimfull – and there is some circumstantial evidence to back this up.)

Jane Bowles frequented Dean's from 1948. But in 1954 William Burroughs, possibly due to his drugs notoriety (he was "Morphine Minnie" to the Tangier police), claimed that he had received a hostile reception there from a 'horrible vista of loud-mouthed, red-faced drunks'.

Dean's Bar, with its boy dancers, is definitely the setting for the opening chapter of Robin Maugham's "The Wrong People"– although it's called "Wayne's bar" in the book. (It is reckoned to be one of the best gay thrillers of all time, although he was *not* popular with other Tangerinos for writing it, nor with his famous uncle Somerset Maugham.) In those days Dean's Bar may have been L-shaped, with another room, probably for the boy dancers, opening out at the back to the right – but this extra space later disappeared.

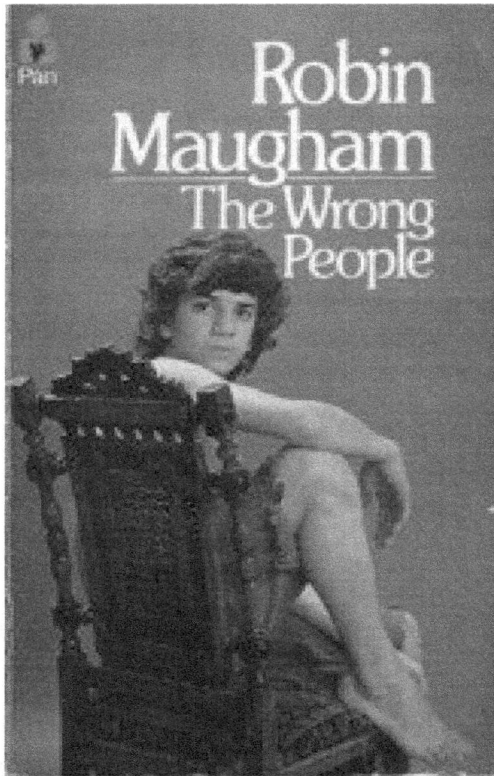

The opening scene of this novel is set in Dean's Bar

During the 1950s Dean's had been handy for users of the British Post Office which was then situated across the street. In addition it was near to a wine merchants, which tended to be a very important facility for expats in a Muslim country! It was also close to Minzah's nightclub, at 31 Amerique du Sud, a building which had started life as the French consulate and later became the Piano Bar [19].

Peter Lacey, a one-time lover of the artist Francis Bacon, played the piano there in the late fifties, and the Woolworth heiress Barbara Hutton met a new lover, Lloyd Franklin, in June 1960, not actually in the bar but when he was a singer-guitarist there. At that time the bar had become known internationally, and it was described by several people as being superbly run. Dean himself was considered a most amusing conversationalist, full of local information, gossip and scandal, and an entry in 'Edmonds Guide to Tangier 1960' is worth quoting in full:

"'Dean' – that is a name that you might hear if you were to ask a member of the British Colony to nominate Tangier's leading citizen. Dean has lived some twenty years in Tangier and for more than half this time has conducted his own bar . This has become one of the meeting places of the International Set. Titled people rub shoulders with smugglers. In the back lounge one may sit within panelled walls and browse through 20-year-old Tatlers and Illustrated London News. Beverley Nichols, Dawn Adams, Margaret Leighton, Alec Waugh and Lady Diana Cooper all drop in from time to time.

"Amazingly, during the war Germans, Italians, Spanish, Japanese, British, Americans and French (both Vichy *and* Gaullist), all frequented the bar." It is said that the usual friendly, relaxed atmosphere prevailed even during the war, and among such wildly improbable fellow-drinkers!

(*Ed.*: In case the last paragraph is starting to remind readers of the film "Casablanca" with its Rick's Bar, there is one theory that the story which inspired the film was really set in Tangier, but that the film-makers called it "Casablanca" as it sounded more romantic. So maybe the many tourists who visited Casablanca hoping to find Rick's Bar were looking in the wrong city?)

Some years later, prolific writer Rupert Croft-Cooke, ever a cynic, described Dean as 'mean and grasping' and he certainly had that reputation, despite being such a good talker. But even Croft-Cooke

---

[19] You will later read a strange story about the Piano Bar in Chapter 27, Unusual Tangier Doctors.

had a soft spot for Dean and he attended his funeral after he sadly died suddenly in 1963, being buried close to his famous bar at St Andrew's Church.

The hole-in-the-wall entrance is still there and the bar still functions. As we mentioned, in later years it lost its wider space at the back where the boy dancers had performed. It was certainly not very appealing when I visited in 1993 with a young Tanjawi friend: just a small space behind a bead curtain, a Tangier bar like any other...

But what memories were held within those four walls!

Thousand and One Nights

From perhaps the least luxurious bar to one of the most...

This remarkable establishment was said to have served the finest food ever presented in a restaurant/bar in Morocco. It was opened, at the suggestion of an American couple, John and Mary Cooke, in a narrow wing of the run-down half-century old Menebhi family's palace on the Marshan cliff, opposite the Italian consulate. It had formerly been the harem quarters of the palace, built by Mehdi el-Menebhi, the war minister of former Sultan Abd el-Aziz.

The Menebhi Palace in the Kasbah, part of which became 1001 Nights

Its address was 22 Rue Assad ibn al Farrat, but as it was in the Kasbah area it was a bit remote from the Ville Nouvelle where most of the expats lived. The restaurant became famous, however, when it was run by American artist Brion Gysin, who was later a literary friend of William Burroughs and to whom he had been introduced by Paul Bowles. He called the restaurant the 'Mil y Una' (Thousand and One Nights).

Gysin furnished the 1001 with red-tiled wooden tables and comfortable banquettes, huge brass candle holders and intricate brass lanterns. The menu was on a burned wooden tablet. There was a vast fireplace and Gysin's own paintings of North African desert scenes adorned the walls.

He opened the restaurant in early 1954.

Brion Gysin visiting Asilah, shortly after opening Tangier's 1001

In addition to the celebrated Moroccan food, Gysin was very proud to showcase Mohamed Hamri's Master Musicians of Jajouka, as well as fire-eaters, acrobats and 12 to 14-year old dancing boys. Local journalist David Woolman described the scene:

'As the orchestra burst into sound...a dancing boy came bolting down the salon with a large, round brass tray, holding six to ten glasses of tea and a lighted candle, balanced on his head...managed to writhe to the floor as the music almost died away, lie prone except for his head's balancing the laden tray, and somehow contrive to turn completely over...slowly regain his feet, and to a crescendo of music and applause, fly from the room...'

It was fashionable not only with expats (especially gays) but also with more prosperous Moroccans. It flourished in 1955, when Tangier was otherwise going through a difficult period with the struggle for independence, but it had to close at the end of March 1956 as Gysin decided to travel.

It reopened in summer 1957 when he returned, but there were difficulties with the suspicious and hostile Moroccan staff, and eventually Mary Cooke took over from Gysin in 1958. Ownership passed later to chef Elizabeth David's husband Tony, and a rich eccentric Englishman called John Torr took over the day-by-day running of it.

In 1960 the restaurant advertised itself as follows:

'In the harem quarters of an ancient palace, to the music of a Riffian orchestra and dancing, enjoy a memorable dinner at the 1001 Nights, Tangier's internationally best-known Moroccan restaurant.'

The Parade

Now a bar not quite as luxurious as the 1001, but even more popular.

Two Americans, a tall, handsome southerner called Jay Haselwood and a suave New Yorker chef named Bill Chase, together with the Russian Ira Belline, had a chance encounter in Rabat with the eccentric Countess Phyllis de la Faille. The latter owned a house in Tangier said to be filled with countless animals and birds. Her house with so many animals was not too hygienic, and she suggested they should open, at her expense, a high-class restaurant in Tangier to give her somewhere up-to-standard to eat.

They followed her command, and the Parade opened in the Rue de Fes in 1946. The rented premises had been completely renovated, and the Woolworth heiress Barbara Hutton and Tangier artists James and Marguerite McBey were at the opening night. But although the restaurant was widely admired, the partners, not altogether surprisingly, fell out and it closed in those premises.

Six months later, however, Haselwood re-established the Parade, this time at 35 Rue des Vignes (now Avenue Prince Heritier), across from the Mauritania cinema and up from the Hotel Atlas.

Although small and inconspicuous in an arcade, its interior featured a jet-black bar and contrasting white floor, red plush curtains and three large shiny oil paintings depicting half-naked Nubian adolescents rowing Venetian gondolas!

At the rear was a small paved garden with, at different times, a resident parrot, an owl and a cockatoo. Rupert Croft-Cooke later made marmalade from its solitary orange tree.

English and American expats and visitors made the Parade their "headquarters", and it was featured in several US magazines. It was open from 7pm and specialised in steaks and light suppers. Local journalist David Woolman thought it one of the best place to dine in all northern Morocco, and he would certainly have known.

The owner, Jay Haselwood, by the way, was nicknamed "Radio Tangier" by Woolman, since he always knew and "broadcast" the latest news about the other expats. (Although perhaps Woolman himself could have competed for the same title!)

The Parade Bar in Tangier, with Jane Bowles on the left, Dean of Deans's Bar holding a glass and Rupert Croft-Cooke on the right

On the other hand Burroughs and Capote were very scathing about the place – whether it was because they were made unwelcome there, one cannot be sure. Burroughs described it as 'stocked with the dreariest breed of piss-elegant cagy queens', although this didn't discourage him from eating there. Haselwood made a fortune from serving martinis and jumbo hamburgers to homesick Americans. According to Truman Capote, however, he also "served up the asses of Arab lads and lasses". But no one else corroborated this last opinion.

Jane Bowles patronised the bar in 1948 at special prices, including free food, as she was short of money at the time. She continued to visit for the next 20 years, until her mental decline led her to start giving away her (and Paul's) money to strangers

Paul Lund (left) and friends at the Parade, including Haselwood (right)

The Parade flourished under Haselwood until he tragically died of a heart attack, aged only 48, on Christmas Day 1965. He was buried at St Andrew's Church.

The restaurant was taken over by a Swiss-French woman called Lily Wickman who reputedly had previous experience as – wait for it – a lion-tamer and a Wall of Death motor cycle rider. Wow!

She got Brion Gysin to draw on the tablecloths, which she framed and hung on the walls. She was probably the 'Lily' who in 1967 charged Kenneth Williams 45 dirhams for a meal. ("Daylight robbery!" he exclaimed in his usual dramatic way.)

Sadly Lily died and the bar closed. The whole block was redeveloped soon afterwards, and regrettably nothing now remains. (Moroccans often do not preserve the places which might appeal most to tourists – elegant, historic or attractive old buildings are sadly sometimes demolished and replaced by bland modern ones.) Yet during the 1960s the Parade and its near neighbour, Trudy Gardo's Viennese Bar, had been considered the two very best places, amongst both Moroccans and the expats, for a wonderful night out – as well as for meeting some of the most illustrious people.

Bar La Mar Chica and Bar Pasapoga

Until about 1950, Tangier's night life had revolved around the Socco Chico and in particular the Café Central, which had featured such delights as a resident orchestra made up of Englishwomen who called themselves the 'Hungarian Rhapsodians'.

But this Medina area, especially after dark, became dangerous for Europeans, so nocturnal entertainment moved down to the harbour area, near to the station.

The English writer Rupert Croft-Cooke describes the Bar La Mar Chica for us: "I like gypsies and flamenco dancing and singing and what is unfairly called 'low life.' I find myself more often than not (at night) in a bar, once a ship-chandler's store, near the port… It consists of a low, narrow room painted in a very ugly dark green, with shuttered windows looking on to a narrow pavement. Behind the long counter stands Paco, flanked by two young Moors, and the proprietor Adolfo stands near the door. The customers are of every Tangerine category…"

William Burroughs was another regular. He described it in 1954 as an "all-night bar where everybody goes after midnight… the proprietor of Mar Chica looks like an 1890 ex-prize fighter, a bit fat, but still a man of great strength and exceedingly evil disposition. A beautiful Arab boy serves behind the bar – every queer has propositioned him, but he won't play."

Robin Maugham reported that the bar itself was a long slab of marble with a mirror on the wall behind; there was sawdust on the floor and fluorescent lighting. Opinions, in fact, rather varied about the bar. American journalist David Woolman wrote that it was the rendezvous after midnight where you could pick up a companion of any persuasion to sleep with at the wink of an eye, and he would have known. He called it a clap-trap badly lit little bar, run by a Spaniard who had fought against Franco.

Bar La Mar Chica was near where the people are looking down, opposite station, c.1958. (Note how the town was starting to grow).

Cyril Connolly called it 'a desultory place...the ultimate station of the lost'. Burroughs' boy friend Kiki loved hanging out at Bar la Mar Chica, as did Paul Bowles' protégé Mohammed Mrabet, who told the story of how he was picked up there by an Englishman for a sex party. Disgraceful.

English Tangier-resident and head of the social set David Herbert, on the other hand, gave Bar la Mar Chica a rather good account, although one is surprised that he didn't consider it too down-market. (*Ed.* Perhaps it reminded him of 1920s Berlin where he had lived and visited nightclubs as a young man, having been taken there by a sympathetic uncle. Both cities, Berlin in the 20s and Tangier in the 50s, acted as magnets for poorer youths/young men from surrounding regions, and both cities seem to have created these cabaret type of bars, where young men on the lookout were often as welcome as older gentlemen, maybe also on the lookout.)

Here is Herbert's description of Bar la Mar Chica: "Before going to bed at about 4am, we would go to the Mar Chica, a little Spanish bar near the port, with sawdust on the floor and wobbly wooden tables and chairs. Here you found flamenco dancers and singers performing to an upright piano, a violin, a guitar and the clicking of castanets…

"Apart from the professionals employed there, individuals would get up impromptu and perform…Carmella was one of the permanent attractions. A middle-aged Spanish gipsy with a flat, Slavic face, possessed a certain charm…a star in her day, now reduced to singing in this bar."

Herbert was noted for his quick wit and repartee, as on one occasion he visited the Mar Chica bar. His guest was a visiting English lady, and when a Spanish transvestite came on the stage, the guest whispered to him, "Mr Herbert, is that a Jack or a Jill?"

"No, dear," he replied, "that's the pail of water."

Follow the arrow down to lowest buildings – that was the location of Bar la Mar Chica, opposite the station and docks

Woolman says that the Mar Chica had by around 1960 been pushed into second place as the Tangerinos' favourite late-night choice by the Pasapoga. This was situated in the Rue de Fes, opposite the Cinema Le Paris., in the arcade next to the Fine Bouche liquor store and supermarket (still there).

The Pasapoga was run by a man named Dowell Jones, an ageing Welshman with a glass eye. Woolman tells us that Jones admired "Spanish and Moroccan boys, entertained them constantly in wholesale lots, and enjoyed life immensely. Owning a fine voice and a resounding laugh, Jones competed with a large number of other (expat) men , but he certainly ranked as their uncrowned king when it came to numbers." He had run a successful Putney auction business and now lived well in Tangier apartments, able to pursue his interests publicly for years.

In due course, however, Dowell Jones came to grief with Authority, and even then only because his juvenile friends got to urinating in the corridors of whatever apartment building he was in! The Pasapoga became the successful centre of a call-boy industry and lasted for several years before it was eventually raided and closed...

Joe Orton was introduced to Dowell Jones in May 1967 by George Greaves[20]. Joe recorded in his diary that Jones was reputed to be *persona non grata* in England. "George said, 'He looks like a frog and has only one eye. He takes it out, you know. I remember once I was having dinner with him and he took it out and wiped it. It slipped from his hand and fell straight into the pudding'."

Croft-Cooke found that the clientele in the early 1950s had been mainly opportunistic young Spaniards, as the name of the bar, Pasapoga, rather suggests. He noted, however, that as the years went by, the Spanish young men in both bars were gradually being replaced by Moroccan dock workers.

The Mar Chica and the Pasapoga closed their doors in the mid to late 1960s, a loss not only to tourists but also to the expat residents, as well as to the remaining young Spaniards.

---

[20] There is more about George Greaves on pages 173-174.

22
Angus Stewart
by *Paul Horler and Alan Moriarty*

Author Angus Stewart, who visited/lived in Tangier in the 1960s

Paul begins: Angus, the son of distinguished novelist J.I.M. Stewart (who also went under the name of Michael Innes for his crime stories), was himself a very promising writer. He grew up in Belfast and later in Oxford, where his father was a lecturer in English at Christ Church – Angus eventually studied under him.

He first stayed in Tangier in late 1961 when he lived in very basic accommodation.. He was to spend part of each year thereafter in Tangier, staying at various addresses including the penthouse in the Loteria building [21] in Rue Delacroix in sight of Café Metropole.

---

[21] author William Burroughs also stayed there at a different time, in 1964.

He established some kind of friendship with the Bowles, and he stayed for a while at their Immeuble Itesa flat, near the American embassy, when the couple returned to New York for a while.

Fame really came for Angus with the publication of "Sandel" in 1968. (Indeed, one of Angus' reasons for going to Tangier was probably to make contact with the many fellow writers out there.) This was the story of a relationship between an undergraduate and a choir school head boy which, unbelievably by today's standards and given the subject, was both critically well received and a best seller!

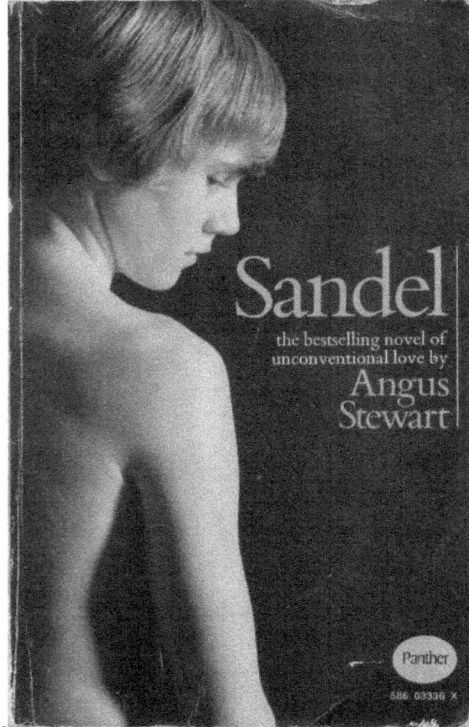

"Sandel" sub-titled "the bestselling novel of unconventional love".[22]

I was deeply affected by reading this novel, so much so that I wrote to the author via the publisher. We met in London and were to become quite close for a while.

---

[22] see critics' favourable reviews on page 138

Angus took me to his parents' home near Wantage, where he had his own bungalow in the grounds. By this time, 1969, his second novel had been published, called "Snow in Harvest". It was a complex spy story and not as popular as "Sandel." It was set partly in Tangier, and deserved to have been better regarded than it was by the critics of the time. (One rather touching part, based on truth, is where an Englishman takes a young Moroccan to the cinema and sees a film with the usual romance and kissing between the sexes. After the film the young man asked his older friend "Why do they never show people like us kissing in films?").

His father's book "Myself and Michael Innes" is, despite including some family photos with Angus in them, curiously reticent about his son. Yet the author Paul Bowles makes references to Angus in his collected letters called "In Touch", where the Foreword contains an acknowledgement of Angus' work.

Alan Moriarty continues:

I first met Angus Stewart in about 1969 when we were both visiting a mutual friend in London. I found him a most relaxed and amiable character whom I liked from the outset. He was living part-time in Tangier then, and was rather fond of the local *kif.* He had a little pipe filled with the stuff and was puffing at it regularly.

Several years passed before we met again, when we somehow agreed to meet in my regular evening haunt of that time, El Camino just off Soho Square. He was at that time working on his book "Tangier: a Writer's Notebook" and he showed me a folder of photos he was thinking about putting in.

From then on we got on very well, with Angus coming up to town regularly and staying with me on each occasion. I also stayed at his house in Wantage, where Angus's main occupation at that time was keeping hedgehogs. (His father was very helpful with the research I was doing at the time into Lewis Carroll, allowing me access to the library of Christ Church Oxford, of which he was a member and where Angus had been an undergraduate).

Later, however, my encounters with Angus were to become more worrying because of his deteriorating health. He made another trip to Tangier when very unfit, and a family member had to fly out and arrange for his return, followed by hospitalisation in the UK.

I saw him for the last time in 1987 when he was in a fairly deteriorated state. The signs were not good, and I am told he has since passed away.

Reactions to Angus Stewart's first
novel *Sandel*

Here is a controlled and beautifully written
love story . . . this is a superb stylistic feat.
New Statesman

Mr Stewart has really succeeded with this
young character, and in depicting a love which
truly exists and is not despicable.
Sunday Telegraph

The writing is always intelligent, its sensual
quality surprisingly beautiful.
The Times

. . . Controlled writing; often funny . . . the
whole thing adds up to a remarkably good
first novel.
The Observer

. . . Mr Stewart is a coolly witty writer, and . . .
offers a great deal of promise for the future.
Sunday Times

Back to Paul to finish :
Just for the record, Angus had four books to credit: "Sandel", "Snow In Harvest" and "Tangier, a writer's notebook". The fourth was a slim volume of verse "Sense and Inconsequence", published in 1972 with an introduction, rather excitingly, by none other than W.H. Auden! There were also illustrations by "Meti", one of his Tangier friends. The BBC broadcast some of the verses.

He won the Richard Hillery award for literature with three of his short stories, two of which had appeared in the London Magazine and were later published in 1964 by Faber & Faber. His work also featured in "Best Horror Stories Two" published by Faber, 1965, and another in a collection entitled "Scottish Tales of Terror."

23
The Hotel Muniria

*This research on Tangier's Hotel Muniria
and its famous guest is by Paul Horler*

The Muniria: the crenellated white building, variously described as being in the old French or Spanish part of Tangier, is on a steep slope above the harbour. It has two storeys plus two patio roof apartments at the higher end. It used to have a lower ground floor section at the lower end, which is now the Tanger Inn. Next to it is a small garden containing a tall palm tree, adjoining Rue Cook. The hotel and bar entrances are at the side, in Rue Magellan.

A 1921 map shows the site empty, but I believe the Muniria does date from the early 1920s, and it may have been a pension from the start. I have not seen any written references prior to 1955 but it can be seen (distantly) on several postcards in my collection from the mid-1920s onwards.

The Hotel Muniria, Tangier, on a hill above the port

The Muniria is packed full of history and the number of famous people who have stayed there is extraordinary. Just for starters, Francis Bacon (1909–92), the Irish-born British painter, stayed at the Muniria in the summer of 1955. It was at that time recalled by one visitor as a 'modest but well-kept place run by a Vietnamese woman who was said to have been "a madame in Saigon". Bacon apparently returned for brief visits in 1956–9.

View across the bay from one of the Muniria bedrooms

American writers William Burroughs (1914–97) and David Woolman moved to the Villa Muniria in late 1955, with their rooms costing just fifteen dollars a month. They had found that their former address at 'Dutch Tony's' in the Medina had become unsafe due to nationalist disturbances brought about by the exiling by the French of Sultan Mohammed V (who later returned to became king in 1957).

On arrival at the Muniria Burroughs and Woolman found that a British minor criminal called Paul Lund (1914–66) was already living at the hotel. He ran the notorious Bar Navarra in the Ville Nouvelle and was dubbed the 'Smiling Damned Villain', Tosh Mundy [23] in the book by Rupert Croft-Cooke.

Burroughs and Woolman finally took the two top apartments, rooms 7 and 8. But the former was often drunk or under the influence of drugs – nearly falling off the top terrace – so he was he was moved to an apartment just off the basement garden.

---

[23] There is a photo of him on page 130

Another explanation may have been that the tolerant landlady ('you can be free here, you understand.') might nonetheless have preferred to keep any unseemliness off the hotel stairs!

It was in the garden room, room 9 and later the Tanger Inn, that Burroughs was to write The Naked Lunch, published in 1959. Explaining to a friend, US writer Allen Ginsberg (who had just come back from a trip to Algeria) about his move to the Muniria, he wrote: "Spot of landlady bother at the old place. She tells me to slack off the Arab visitors. So me and Dave Woolman...have found us the original 'anything goes' joint run by two retired junky whores from Saigon.

"On the ground floor are Dave, myself and 'Calamity Kate' Gifford [24], a colourful Englishman....with our rooms opening on the garden. We have a private entrance...my part is one room and one bed, generally cluttered up with Spanish boys." (Over 18s for Burroughs.)

It was this basic small white-washed room with its shower alcove, wardrobe and gas burner, which was said to have been accurately represented in Cronenberg's film 'The Naked Lunch'. The film also depicted Burroughs seeing phaluses coming out of his typewriter – and for this reason throwing it out of the Muniria window, when he was in an upstairs room.

Burroughs would sometimes take the orgone box [25] into the garden, where the hotel's two cats were. But for the most part his daily routine consisted of :- during the day rowing in the bay and writing, then in the evening drinking/eating out with Woolman and Gifford. In his book "William Burroughs: El Hombre Invisible," Barry Miles wrote: Bill covered one wall of his room entirely from photographs, mostly from his 1953 jungle expedition... Another wall, pitted with bullet-holes, was used as his shooting gallery. He built an orgone accumulator in one corner of the room and would sit doubled up in it, smoking *kif*."

---

[24] There is a section about Calamity Kate Gifford in the next chapter.

[25] The Orgone box or Orgone accumulator was a kind of alternative therapy of the day; the gadget was supposed to generate energy and to have aphrodisiac properties. It was also considered to alleviate post heroin sickness. Orgone therapy was in due course discredited and its originator , Wilhelm Reich, imprisoned for misrepresentation.

In 1957 American author-composer and long-term Tangier resident Paul Bowles (1910–99) described Burroughs' room in the Muniria: 'there were hundreds of pages of yellow foolscap all over the floor, month after month, with heel prints on them, rat droppings, bits of old sandwiches, sardines. It was filthy.'

View from Burroughs' window, overlooking Sacré Coeur Church

US/Canadian writer Jack Kerouac (1922–69) stayed there in room 7 in February to April 1957, paying $20 a month for a room '...with a red tile patio overlooking the sea...' But even for him it became too extreme – with the serene Sacré Coeur church on the one side of his patio and on the other a Dutchman bringing young Arabs back to his room night after night. "On the roof," he said "there was a French landlady chatting to a Chinese housekeeper, and down below Burroughs sat typing wild-haired in his garden apartment – he had a kerosene stove, but luckily he didn't set fire to the whole place!"

To add to the fun, Burroughs was joined in March by American 'beat' poet Allen Ginsberg (1926–97) and his friend Peter Orlovsky, who in April moved into Kerouac's vacated room, 'Jack's old veranda great room overlooking bay and Spain'. They did not stay long but they did help to collate Bill's writing.

But Burroughs was becoming tired of the Tangier scene. He spent the summer of 1957 in Denmark and left the Muniria in

January 1958, going to the 'Beat Hotel' in Paris. He said he had become alarmed at the Dutchman and his endless activities with teenage boys – although he would return. Bowles' protege, the Moroccan painter Ahmed Yacoubi (1931–79) stayed there in the summer of 1958, lying low to avoid the police homosexual purge.

Burroughs returned to his old room in April 1961, together with two more young English acolytes, Ian Sommerville and Michael Portman. A reunion took place that summer when Ginsberg, Orlovsky and US poet Gregory Corso came to Tangier and stayed in the even cheaper (lower down the same hill) Hotel Armor at 26 rue Magellan. It was Corso who nicknamed the Muniria, not inappropriately, the 'Villa Delirium'!

Ansen liked it so much he stayed there in the summers of '62 and '63. A photo session with him included took place in the garden of the Muniria where they all gathered, together with Paul Bowles.

In the Muniria garden: from left to right: Peter Orlovski, Burroughs, Ginsberg, Alan Ansen, Bowles (seated), Gregory Corso, Ian Somerville

Burroughs and his two young friends, who were assisting with the preparation of his latest book, moved in July 1963 to 4 Calle Larache, in the Marshan district – they had little option as they were awaiting the arrival in Tangier of Burroughs' son Billy.

The lad, aged sixteen, lived with them for about six months altogether. But Billy eventually abandoned the effort to get on with his father and he returned to the USA. Burroughs himself left there finally – to stay for a while at the penthouse flat of the Loteria building, which had been occupied in 1962 by Angus Stewart.

The Muniria was then taken over by a British gay couple, the eccentric John Sutcliffe and his friend Peter Tuckwell. One change they made was the opening of the Tanger Inn in the section adjoining the garden in 1965, and the hotel slowly became less outrageous than it had been with Woolman and Burroughs.

Bowles' Moroccan protégé, the writer Mohammed Mrabet (b.1935) was barman at the Tanger Inn in 1965 and caught Yacoubi trying to leave the hotel without paying. He based his story 'Love with a Few Hairs' on those experiences.

Moroccan Abdul Jayou was another close friend of Sutcliffe (although there was no jealousy between him and Peter – who had become very ill), and he helped him run the Muniria. Both the Britons have now died and Abdul Jayou may have taken over the hotel from Sutcliffe in the late 80s. Abdul had already married and he lived there with his wife, who helped him run the hotel very ably.

Wind the clock forward to about 2001, and Brian Ronson tells me that on a nostalgia holiday to the Muniria he noticed that Abdul Jayou's son Hamza had become a fine, strapping youth and an expert at finding taxis for guests. Hamza had kindly taken Brian's case up to his room for him but left it quickly at the door – before he had the chance of being chatted up or even tipped! No doubt his father had warned him against getting involved with friendly guests.

Brian experienced a second disappointment when he went next door for a drink at the Tanger Inn: a group of good looking young Moroccans lads came in, dressed up in elegant and rather (he thought) camp gear, so his heart leapt.

A short time later, however, the door opened and some equally good looking Moroccan girls entered, also dressed up to the nines. Poor Brian was of course ignored by both groups. A friend later told him that modern Moroccan lads dress up in what we'd call a rather camp style (laquered hair, white trousers and jewellery, etc.) when they're chasing girls. So Brian realised the Tanger Inn was still a "no questions asked" kind of place. The trouble was that both the question and answer had changed from when he'd first visited Tangier in its heyday.

The Rough Guide of several editions described the hotel as friendly and excellent value. There were eight rooms available in 2006, little altered from the 1950s. A single room there was remarkably inexpensive (around ten pounds a night), when you consider the amount of history that had taken place within its walls and how they could have exploited the fact.

A last view of the Muniria, from the hotel opposite

24
Three Elegant Gentlemen

Justin Dark by *Alan Moriarty*

A noteworthy visitor to Tangier was Justin Dark, a travel writer, who arrived in the grand style, followed by a small train of local porters carrying his leather suitcases. Justin, son of a rich and distinguished family, had from boyhood single-mindedly devoted himself to scattering his inheritance to the four winds, and further. In Tangier he stayed with two old friends (one being myself) in a large seafront apartment.

The last stage of his journey had been in the ramshackle train from Asilah which in those days ran along Tangier beach. It was later learned that Justin had been observed leaning out of the train from his first class carriage and waving to the young bathers.

A train coming along Tangier beach always caused great excitement

At that time, Justin had no fixed address, but moved from one expensive hotel to another. His travels appeared to have had something of the quality of a royal progress, since trains, buses and ferries were constantly being held up while the porters whom Justin had demanded were sought. But he was not so unpopular as one might think, since he tipped with reckless abandon.

In the present earnest-minded day, it might be said that Justin had an 'alcohol issue'. But in those days, it was simply noted that he was of an extremely convivial disposition – and not the only one, in that time and place.

On arrival, Justin announced that the following day was his birthday. He added his view that, on a birthday, the celebrant should treat others, rather than himself be treated. No objection was raised to this, so Justin, like Socrates in his final hours, prepared to call his friends [26] around him to celebrate his long and eventful life.

Throughout the morning, choice dishes, cakes, fruits and desserts arrived at the apartment, together with more than enough alcohol to float a transatlantic liner. Mention here could particularly be made of the 2-litre bottles of self-proclaimed Scotch sold in a discreet corner of the local supermarket, and which had caught Justin's eye.

We pass over the scenes of revelry that followed. Suffice it to say that, in the small hours of Sunday morning, peace eventually fell on the apartment block. But not for long – since, around 3 am, the silence of the area was rudely shattered by a fearful uproar emanating from the apartment where Justin was staying – banging, rattling, cries of pain and distress. In short, Justin had locked himself in the loo.

Bit by bit, a small crowd of Justin's friends gathered outside the door, uttering little squeaks of concern and offering conflicting advice. Screwdrivers were poked into the lock and twisted, oil was dribbled into it, but the key, which had become damaged in some way, obstinately refused to turn.

In the end Justin's friends faced the inevitable, and a young runner was sent for the nearest locksmith. He arrived with commendable speed and, with equal speed and a 'snick', the door was opened, releasing the astonishing apparition of a much dishevelled Justin in a voluminous white nightshirt.

---

[26] Another of his friends being Horace Gendell, who has contributed to several chapters in this Tangier section.

In fairness to Justin, though, he generously insisted on paying the locksmith,who departed with considerably more than the (already outrageous) sum he had asked for. Not however before pointing out that – forgotten by the apartment's owners and unnoticed by Justin – a spare key hung just inside the door, against precisely this kind of emergency.

It was said that the story of the locksmith was re-told over many a pot of tea at the cafés on the Rue Pasteur. By the time it had, after several retellings, reached the Windmill and BBC Café on the beach, it was related that all three queens, not just one, had been locked in the loo and that their screams had been heard as far away as the Petit Socco! Is there no truth any more?

Astonishingly, Justin is still alive and well at the time of writing (2008), and living in the Far East, where his adventures – and misadventures – regularly furnish copy for the local newspapers. On the last occasion I had met him, several years ago, he shook his head sadly over Tangier and doubted whether he would ever return, as there were 'too many lunatics' there.

I could only agree and sympathise.

Calamity Kate & Sir Alvary by *Adrian Hammond*

An earlier and elegant Tangerino called Eric Gifford (1906–1978) earned the nickname of 'Calamity Kate', owing to a series of disasters which befell him in Tangier.

Having first taken up residence there in the 1930s, he left Tangier in World War II – of which more later. But at the end of the war he came back, naturally wanting to visit the villa he had had built for him just before the war. On his way he called in to see some friends in Dean's Bar, where they swopped news. He then mentioned that he was going up to see the villa – but noticed them passing each other a strange look.

Twenty minutes later he returned to the bar looking very crestfallen. "But it's gone!" he said. (During his absence locals had not only taken the contents but every brick and tile of the villa too.)

In later years he used to stay at the Muniria, deciding that a hotel would be less likely to disappear during his absences. He also found a very useful paid job there – looking after William Burroughs at the Muniria during his drug sprees and making sure he took meals, changed his clothes and didn't fall out of the window. Even later than that, he became a columnist in Madrid, so he did finally find a successful life for himself.

Another calamity for him had occurred much earlier, however, actually at the start of World War Two, when Tangier was occupied by the Spanish army. He was living near the Villa Harris (Walter Harris' former house) on the outskirts of Tangier. About half a dozen handsome and muscular Spanish soldiers were billeted in it, and they noted with some interest that Calamity was "the only gay in the village." He for his part noticed how glum and lonesome they all looked, separated from their women-folk, and he formed a clever plan to stiffen up their morale, and maybe something else too.

One day, meeting some of them near to a barn, in which he had everything prepared ready for such an emergency, he did his usual routine of smiling at them all amiably, one hand on hip and pouting his lips, looking them up and down (mainly down) but this time pointing in the direction of the barn. The hint was taken and they all quietly went inside the building, where Calamity generously offered himself to the lonely infantrymen.

Unfortunately, or maybe fortunately, he was only halfway through servicing the line of troops when it was brought to a sudden end by an officer who, having noticed Calamity flirting with his men and now hearing strange grunts and groans coming from the barn, decided to investigate. Seeing what was happening he ordered his troops to withdraw their weapons from action – and then had Calamity placed under arrest, since he was sure it was all his fault..

However, that left the Spanish with a big problem. You see General Franco had abolished sodomy in Spain before the war, so such a thing could theoretically not have happened, now could it? – least of all inside the new model Spanish army.

For this reason the soldiers were just reprimanded for trespassing in the farmer's barn and, as the officer felt Calamity had instigated the matter, he was charged with the serious (but much more respectable) offence of being a spy.

Oh dear…Calamity might well have spent the rest of the war behind bars had not His Majesty's rep. in Tangier, with the wonderful name of Sir Alvary de Gascoigne (our third elegant gentleman), heard rumours about the charge. He just would not accept that an Englishman could possibly be involved in spying – until it was whispered in his ear what had really happened.

"But that's fifty times worse!" he gasped.

Sir Alvary feared that if word of this scandal got out, it could crack the moral fibre of the British Empire more effectively than Hitler's Luftwaffe. So he managed to persuade the Tangier authorities to set the prisoner free, which they agreed to do but on condition that he left Tangier immediately.

Calamity was released from jail and set off for the West Indies, although after the war he decided to slip back into Tangier again, guessing rightly that everyone by then would have forgotten his small moral lapse.

He arrived back in Tangier – bright-eyed, bushy-tailed, and really looking forward to seeing his villa again.....Poor Calamity.

25
Five cheerful Tangerinos
byTim Vaughan and Adrian Hammond

Tim Vaughan starts: The first of the cheerful Tangerinos arrived in Tangier in the latter years of Calamity Kate. He was a colourful character, coming dramatically onto the scene and making an instant mark. It was the young **Rowan Tudor**, a Scotsman by birth who, with his red hair, flowing red beard and, above all, his *kilt* guaranteed he was quickly noticed on the streets of Tangier.

The kilt was the source of endless fascination amongst the locals, since they had never seen one before and they would sometimes ask for firm evidence of his manhood – refused, naturally. (The kilt was also a "passe-partout" since, whenever he hitched a ride with it on, he was 100% certain to be picked up!).

Editor: Rowan deserves a special tribute from us all, as he knew the "scene" so well in Tangier and in other locations, and we are grateful to him for all his information. He also persuaded Peter Kendall to make his excellent contribution.

When you are chatting to Rowan, one just has to remember fascinating titbits he tells you: e.g. mentioning that on the bus in Marrakech he used to see Emma Freud and her two daughters, the characters in the wonderful book and film called "Hideous Kinky". Or mentioning that he once had a coffee in Tangier sitting at the next table to the French gay author Jean Genet.

Or him remembering how one strikingly beautiful youth, whom many expats talked about and drooled over, was nick-named 'Sure-Thing'. They called him that, as they could be absolutely sure of him. (Absolutely sure of him saying "No"!)

Or him recounting how, whilst eating at the restaurant named Chez Larbi he had got into converstion with a Tangier resident named Len Tilley who persuaded him to visit the Parade Bar. At that time the Parade was being run by a lady named Lilly who was playing Viennese music on the piano. Len said, in front of her, at the bar:

"You know, each line on Lilly's face tells a story."

"And such stories," she replied, whimsically.

Back to Tim: Now for our second cheerful character, **Ralph Burton** (codename Rachel). He was indeed a jovial person, always smiling, and his smile always just waiting to break into a laugh.

He used to frequent the BBC Café on the beach, a convivial gathering place for expats in those days. Often young Moroccans would walk along the beach and make assignations through signals to the gentlemen sitting up in the café and looking down at them.

He was enjoying an evening drink at the BBC one summer's day when he made contact with a delightful young Moroccan in this way. So, having met the friend of his dreams, Ralph signalled for him to follow back to his hotel. He was staying at the Hotel Armor, just below the Hotel Muniria at the top of the hill, but he was not too sure whether guests would be allowed in or not. So with the young man in tow, he approached the hotel's night guardian, who had come on duty at eight, with a huge smile.

He placed a packet of cigarettes in the guardian's hands, saying "Pour vous!" Then with an even huger smile he pointed back to his companion and said "Pour moi!"

Laughs all round – and his friend was admitted.

Ralph also became rather expert at keeping prices down – and, if there was any bargaining to do, always winning. One morning he took his jacket to the dry cleaners and as usual asked for a 30% reduction because he was "a regular customer" ("regular" being once a year). The young lady was bowled over by the size of his smile, the sound of his laughter, the strength of his persuasion and by his flashing blue eyes and fair hair – so naturally she agreed.

But he also wanted to have to have the zip on his jacket repaired and, remembering French from his excellent public school, he gave her another of his extra huge smiles, almost a laugh, and asked the attractive young lady: "Vous pouvez faire marcher mon zip?" (Could you get my zip working?). He was more than a little surprised when the young lady rushed round the back and fetched the manager – a large and burly man, who asked him to repeat what he had said.

The manager then explained to Ralph that "zip" was Arabic for penis, so he had inadvertently been asking the young lady to get his private parts working. Again, laughs all round and everyone happy – it always seemed to end that way with Ralph.

Tim now tells us about our third cheerful Tangerino, **Stefan Rogers**, known to many as 'Princess', or occasionally Tuloola. He was to become a veteran of Tangier and Fez, but most especially later on of Agadir.

In all three cities Stefan quickly became a popular figure with the young local Moroccans, although the other gentlemen could not always figure out the secret of that success. He had, it was true, rather the same technique as Calamity Kate Gifford. He would place his hand on his hip, pout his lips and look the Chosen One appreciatively up and down, thus giving him a subtle message of complete compliance with their wishes.

He was not so good, however, at finding accommodation in Tangier and perhaps should have developed some of Ralph's routines. One evening, being followed by a company of adoring worshippers, the leader of whom was called Abdu from Fez, Stefan went up the hill to the cemetery – where three of them took flight for fear of upsetting ancestors, leaving only brave young Abdu and Stefan behind.

But at least it cemented the friendship between them.

There was, by the way, a scurrilous and probably completely fictitious story about Stefan circulating around the beach cafés at this time. He and an English friend (also young and good-looking) were said to have taken a picnic down to the lonely and quiet Atlantic beach, a beach surrounded by bushes and trees.

To their joy they saw they were being followed down the cliff path by a couple of macho and muscular Moroccan admirers, whom they'd made eyes at on the way.

On arrival down in the bushes near the beach – Stefan, his friend and the sandwiches were all, according to the story, thrown to the ground, and the usual ravishment then took place.

Afterwards, safely back on the road, the friend, more shaken than Stefan by the experience, said "You know, they were a bit rough – do you think we should report them to the police?"

"Well, how on earth," replied Stefan, "are we going to explain to the police that we've both been raped twice?"

"But, Stefan, we were only raped once!"

"I know," said Stefan. "But we've got to go back for our sandwiches, haven't we?"

A view of the Atlantic beach from some Tangier ruins

Sensing that neither the Atlantic beach nor the cemetery were ideal, he switched to the main Tangier beach in the evenings for his assignations. He discovered after a few days, however, that the main beach had another snag – the railway. Because the line in those days enclosed the beach like a fence, you could only cross over it at certain points, making it all too easy for bandits to operate. [27]

Needless to say, one evening when his rendezvous had finished and he wanted to go back across the rails, his way was blocked by three powerful young men who demanded a toll fee. Poor Stefan was able to escape only by using all the cheerful charm he could muster – and finally handing over to them his leather jacket.

The incident could have been much worse, but it more or less made up his mind that he should try Fez instead, having heard from Abdu very favourable reports. So he gave the sad news to Abdu that he would soon be leaving.

---

[27] See photo of the line on page 168.

Thus a day or two later Stefan packed his bags, set off for the town station and boarded the train for Fez. Needing to relax after all his adventures, he found a compartment to himself and prepared for a zizz. As the train trundled slowly along the beach, however, the compartment door slid open and who should enter but Abdu!

He explained he'd followed Stefan to the station and smuggled himself on the train, since he was madly in love with him and could not live without him. But (with the sound of the ticket inspector coming down the corridor) he wondered if Stefan could help him with the train fare to Fez – he'd be so eternally grateful.

Adrian Hammond now tells us about our last two cheerful Tangerinos.
Terry Clouter was a cockney, and his gay partner **George**, a geordie. Terry was sharp with a penetrating voice, George laid-back with a calm, deep-pitched one. Terry and George had for some time been the proud owners of a holiday house in Tangier in the smart Marshan area , where they had much enjoyed the social life.

On one occasion they had thrown a rousing party for several dozen Tangerinos and their younger Tanjawi friends. It was financed by their rich friend Arndt Krupp, of the famous German munitions company, who was also a Tangerino and, as readers can imagine, not short of spare cash. "'Chunky Terry and lean Geordie were down to earth, warm friendly and witty," said Woolman. "They were great party-goers, and went everywhere from the finest homes on the Mountain down to the sleaziest bars in the Medina."

In London the couple's job was running a quite successful pub. But on retiring in the 1960s, the couple at last could fulfil their dream of living and working full time in Morocco. Unable, however, to afford the exalted price of a hotel in Tangier, they sold their Tangier holiday home and purchased "a small hotel in Mazagan", having heard very favourable reports of the town. (Mazagan was the old name for el Jadida and the small hotel probably the Provence.)

There they settled down to running the hotel as partners, thoroughly enjoying the social life amongst the other expats and the extremely friendly young locals in el Jadida. During the quieter winter months, when there were fewer guests, they would hold parties at the hotel for all the el Jadida expats. So they soon brought a little of Tangier's sparkle and sociability to their new Moroccan home-town.

Two views of el Jadida (Mazagan) [28]

Sadly it was to last in el Jadida less than five years for the devoted and popular gay couple. George, a diabetic, suddenly died. Poor Terry was totally distraught, sold out and returned to London, where he soon died himself, perhaps of a broken heart. Still, it's nice to know that all their Moroccan days together – first in Tangier, then later in el Jadida – were such happy ones.

---

[28] We hope to include a chapter or two about el Jadida in our next proposed volume (on South Morocco) to be called "Agadir to My Heart."

26
Tales of the Constabulary

Based on interviews with Dudley Short, Ron Nelson (sadly both no longer with us) and with Martin Croydon. Narrated by Tony Walton

By coincidence our fourth, fifth and sixth interviews, with three separate gentlemen who knew old Tangier in its heyday, all threw up tales about the eccentricity of the police in that far-off time.

We would remind readers that these little events occurred around half a century ago, and we are sure cast no reflection whatever on the modern Tangier police.

First the interview with Dudley Short:
Dudley had spent holidays in Tangier several years earlier than Ron Nelson, Martin Croydon or even Rowan Tudor.

When Dudley visited Tangier in the 1950s it was still in its heyday and few felt the need to go further south. I wanted to include this story, as also the one from Peter Kendall, firstly because they are amusing and interesting but secondly because they go back to the days when Tangier was an international zone – so at least ten years even before Joe Orton arrived on the scene.

I had got to know Dudley as he lived in the same Wimbledon street as myself and my ex-soldier, younger partner, Tony Hardy. We were all members of a gay community group of the 1970s and were mutual friends of its founder chairman, Mike Holden, who lived in a flat almost behind Dudley's house. When I first started the research into Tangier/Agadir history I was keen to interview people like Dudley, since obviously they were becoming elderly and frail, but I felt sure they had a tale to tell.

So there we sat, on 21st June 2002, in his cosy back room in South Park Road sipping tea – and the interview began...

First I asked Dudley if he could tell me in which period he used to go on holiday in Tangier. He said that it was around 1954, and I commented I found this quite exciting as he was the very first person I had ever met who had actually *been* there when it was an international zone.

His response was both classic and serious: "Oh. Isn't it still an international zone, then?" Which could go down with the 'Has Mafeking been relieved yet?' series of old stories

What had his first holiday in Tangier been like? Well, he said he vividly remembered arriving at the hotel with his gay friend, to find the manager busy shoo-ing youngish lads away from the door and stopping them pestering tourists. Dudley was glad to see the back of them. He went up to his room, looked out of his balcony – and there they were again!! A line of them in the back alley, looking up at the windows, with their trousers undone and waving their private parts up towards the hotel guests' windows!

Dudley wondered what kind of a place he had come to, he told me. He said he had been hoping to form a deep meaningful relationship with one person, and the lads' behaviour wasn't quite the sort of thing he had in mind.

As an interviewer I must have failed to ask the right kind of question, for apart from the story of his arrival he couldn't seem to remember much about the international zone or its atmosphere. (I've found, in fact, that many of the people from the old days find it very difficult to put recollections into words.) Dudley did eventually, however, tell me the following rather amusing story about the Tangier police in those days:

The tale is really about the gay friend with whom Dudley went on this holiday in 1954. His companion, like Dudley, had no interest in the kind of young layabouts behind the hotel described above, but he just loved anything in a uniform, so he spent the holiday ogling and wanting to chat up every young policeman or soldier he saw, or at least make eyes at him.

Finally two of the policemen could stand it no more, bundled Dudley's friend into a car and took him away to an empty police cell, where, to the great delight of the gentleman concerned, they punished him in a way which aptly suited the crime.

Meanwhile poor Dudley was nearly beside himself with worry, and he was hugely relieved when a police car drew up outside their hotel and a deliriously happy and grateful-looking queen emerged from it.

"Wasn't it thoughtful of them to drive me back afterwards?" was all his friend said, when Dudley told him how frantic he'd been.

Here Dudley seemed to falter in his memories of the holiday, and so I came in with a banal statement like: "Well, at least it livened up the holiday a bit, Dudley!"

"Tony," he replied seriously, "it completely *ruined* the holiday. Because we spent the next ten days tramping round Tangier trying to find those two policemen again."

Now Martin Croydon:
Martin (codename Marcia) visited Marrakech, Tangier and especially Agadir, all during their heydays.

During an early stay in the 1960s he had committed a minor indiscretion behind a palm tree and had been unfortunate enough to be nabbed by a policeman – the other person involved having run away. He was told brutally that he had a stark choice of being taken down to the police-station, or else submitting himself now to the desires of the policeman. (We should perhaps explain that Martin was then a good looking young man and fresh from public school.)

So poor Martin decided he had no option but to think about England and take everything that was coming. Still, at least he was accustomed to the discipline of the dorms.

Unfortunately the policeman took even less care about finding a quiet place than Martin had done five minutes earlier. From his position facing the ground by the road, Martin was horrified to see a Wallace Arnold coach passing, based in the same home county as where he lived, with little old ladies staring in amazement down at the performing couple.

It was only a small compensation afterwards to think that none of the old ladies would have recognised him, having not seen his face from that angle before. But the experience did teach him to find proper accommodation (it turned out to be a small hotel) and to keep to only one or two friends.

Very soon afterwards he started leading a truly monogamous life, forming a loving relationship with a young Moroccan which was happy and uncomplicated. In fact, the only awkward moment was early on in the affair, when one day as they were coming out of a food shop together, a black car drove by. The lad explained that the driver, who had given them both a very friendly wave, was his father.

Martin naturally enough asked what his job was, with a lovely big car like that.

"Papa – assistant chef de police!" replied the lad proudly.

Martin hoped this meant that the lad's father was the assistant head-cook for the local police...but he had an uneasy feeling it meant something else.

Ron Nelson also gave us some memories of the old Tangier days:

When I used to visit Tangier in the 1970s, it was still just about in its heyday, although perhaps starting to creak at the edges.

One of my favourite memories is of how a group of us gentlemen used to meet every morning on the terrace of the Café de Paris for coffee, often to discuss our Moroccan friends – whom we tended to keep on a steady basis for some time.

But on this particular morning a solemn piece of news was brought to us over our coffee. *Catastrophe.* All of our young Moroccan friends had apparently been involved in a fight in a pinball games room, and every one of them had been taken off to jail!

At first we accepted the dreadful news of the arrests with numbness, but as soon as we realised that we were *all* likely to be bereft of our Beloveds, the most militant in our group said "We want our boys back safely, and we're going to go and get 'em back!"

(The phrase "wanting our boys back safely" has a rather nostalgic, war-time, Vera Lynn, ring about it, don't you think?).

"Yes," said someone else "We'll go down to the constabulary now. We want our boys back now, and we won't take 'No' for an answer!"

It was decided that we would all go down as a group and make our bold demand. We devised a cunning plan that at a given signal – me blowing my nose – we would all take a 100 dirham note out of our pockets and hold it nonchalantly against our lapels.

So off went us brave gentlemen down to the constabulary and explained to the officer in charge that we felt our young friends should be discharged and we would accept full responsibility for their future good behaviour.

Not unexpectedly, but very politely, the officer gave us a long-winded speech, something like:

"Thank you for your visit. But it is impossible for the authority to release these young men, since they must be taught a lesson by subjecting them to the very fair and just processes of Moroccan law, which means their case cannot even be heard until the next judicial hearing in November at the earliest…"

At this moment I blew my nose, and each of us discreetly took something from our pockets to hold casually against our lapels.

"On the other hand," continued the officer, very definitely *not* seeming to notice the sudden appearance of so many bank notes, and keeping his eyes fixed downwards, "it may be possible to release them today, owing to a special dispensation of mercy from our gracious king, as it is our beloved majesty's birthday this year."

We were told to wait for them outside the police station, and less than half an hour later we were all re-united with shrieks of joy — but whether these came from our young friends or from us I can't quite remember.

27
Two Tangier Doctors

From unusual policemen to unusual doctors. The first story, told by Brendon Knight[29], is so bizarre it's important to remember it was backed up by several witnesses – few could have invented such a happening.

There was a Scottish expat doctor in 1970s' Tangier who hated gays – nobody knew why. He refused to speak to them or give them any help in his surgery. Newcomers to the town of a certain type were warned by us that on no account were they to go near him.

One evening a group of us fairly open gay men were sitting in the Piano Bar (a known gay venue) and were amazed to see the doctor walk in! He was surprisingly friendly and, astonishingly, gave us all an invitation to a garden party at his grand house on the Mountain. He said he wanted to let bygones be bygones, and to make up for his bad behaviour by giving us a treat and making friends.

Needless to say we were all brimming over with curiosity and couldn't resist the temptation finally to see the house of the man whom up till that moment we had considered a monster.

We decided, understandably, to go together in a group. We very nervously approached the front door, rang the bell and a servant opened it, showing us the way to the doctor's fine garden and onto the lawn, where sherry was distributed liberally. But where was the mysterious doctor himself?

Suddenly the doors of an upstairs balcony opened and the doctor emerged – dressed in a kilt and carrying bagpipes! He proceeded to play a lament, which my friend whispered to me sounded like a cat being strangled, but none of us laughed because we were trying to be polite and build bridges. So when he stopped playing we all clapped and shouted "Encore!"

Whereupon he placed his bagpipes on the ground and reached for something else, and we wondered which musical instrument he would treating us to next. But it wasn't a musical

---

[29] Brendon also contributed three of the short Tunisian tales in Chapter Seven

---

instrument, it was a shotgun! We stood for a moment frozen to the spot wondering, as he aimed it at us, if it was some kind of misplaced joke. Then he began to fire, and we all turned and started running to the gate, thinking our life was about to end, and in blind panic.

We got to the gates but they were locked!! I just can't recollect if we forced them open or found another way out – I just remember the shots went on firing. We ran down the lane and when we were certain we had escaped we realised that none of us had been hit. But whether this was because he was firing blanks or because he was a bad shot we just didn't know…and don't know to this day.

Adrian Hammond now tells us about a much better doctor.
There were many motives for going to live in Tangier, and certainly the gay motive was the biggest one of all. Yet that is not to say that all the Tangerinos led lives of idle self-indulgence, whether gay or straight. Many acts of kindness were performed, and friendship with a European was often a great help to the young Moroccans – e.g. helping them to find work, or helping them with sick relatives.

As we mention elsewhere, the era when we say Tangier was having its heyday was a time of great privation in the region, especially Spain. Dr Hank Tulner in fact did a great deal of good during his years living in Tangier. According to Woolman he gave freely of his help and advice to anyone – native Moroccan, Spanish or others – who approached him.

He was a Dutchman who had been captured by the Japanese in World War II and tortured. But he was unable to settle down to ordinary life in Amsterdam after the war and decided that Tangier was the place to be. A tall kindly man with a ready laugh, Dr Tulner made many friends, not only Tangerinos but also the many Tanjawis (the local Moroccans) for whom he ran a free clinic once a week.

He retired to live in Spain but he would come back to Tangier for his holidays – always a welcome and popular figure.

28
Tangier Diaries
(short extracts selected)

Back in Chapter 16 we gave you a little from the diaries of Jane
Bowles. Here are a few snippets from the Tangier diaries of John
Hopkins, a contemporary of Jane's. His gossipy diary creates a
picture of expat life which often revolved around the Parade Bar:

"Josephine Baker is in town. Last night she performed at one
of the Tangier theatres to raise money for her tribe of orphans. We
went with David Herbert, an old friend of ours...

"Jane Bowles has moved to Hotel Atlas but spends every day
at the Parade Bar handing out drinks and money to every lush in
Tangier...

"Jim Wyllie told us at the Parade that he was walking home
through the Kasbah the other night when a hooded Moroccan
grabbed him from behind, pressed a knife to his jugular and hissed
'Your money or your life!' When Jim cheerfully rebuked him in
Arabic, the would-be assassin stepped back, replying politely, 'Oh, it's
you Mr Wyllie. You may pass.'"

Still on the subject of diaries, how could anyone write about 1960s
Tangier without mentioning Joe Orton and Kenneth Halliwell?

The house in which they stayed, to start with, had a long
history. In it Joe composed part of his diary, but it had been lived in
previously by Tennessee Williams: he wrote his play there, "Suddenly
Last Summer", made into a successful film with Liz Taylor.

The beach where the last very melodramatic scene of
Tennessee Williams' play and film takes place is said to be based on
nearby Asilah. The main character in the play is attacked by the
young men he had been having affairs with, who turn out to be
active cannibals! – a bit unfair on Asilah, where the young men were
said to be kind and gentle[30]. On the other hand Williams could have
heard the sounds of Tangier beach as he wrote the play, so he maybe
he was thinking of that beach too?

---

[30] See Chapter 36: "Trips to Asilah".

Kenneth Williams also at different times stayed in that same quiet Tangier house which Tennessee Williams and Joe Orton (with Kenneth Halliwell) had done.

The secluded Tangier house, stayed in by several famous gays

The Orton Diaries are arguably the most popular gay book ever written. John Lahr's biography, based on them, with the wonderful double-entendre title of "Prick Up Your Ears" was likewise very popular and made into a film.

Our extract from the Tangier section of the Orton diaries dwells neither on his friendship with local lads, nor on the dreadful quarrels with Kenneth Halliwell, but on his friendship with expats – since that's the main theme of this book.

A section of the famous diaries describes his time in Tangier with his partner Kenneth Halliwell, a happy if tense time, at the beginning of the summer in which sadly they were later both to die elsewhere in such tragic circumstances.

From the film "Prick UpYour Ears": just arriving in Tangier.

Our extract is also from this part, dated May 1967. Joe and his partner Kenneth Halliwell are talking to one of the expats of Tangier – the couple seemed always happier and less quarrelsome when they were with a third person:

Went round to the Hotel Mamora, Tangier. It used to be a rendezvous for perverts of all kinds three years ago. Tiresome queens of all nations flocked there. It was then taken over by two English queens from Bournemouth who decided that money lay with virtue rather than vice. They now cater for trippers.

Jimmy said "You've seen that big black thing at the reception desk haven't you?" I nodded. "Well when he came I couldn't cotton on to his name so I called him Lucy. I did this for a fortnight, then he suddenly says: 'No call me Lucy! Lucy no good!'

"I thought, some evil queen has told him it's a girl's name. So I asked him what I should call him. 'No call me Lucy. Call me Rosie.' he replied... So I do!"

Jimmy suddenly kicked up his legs and began to sing:
Fly me to the moon, and let me play among the stars!

(Later) Jimmy took us up to the hotel salon and, dressed only in a pair of brown shorts, flopped onto a chaise-longue. "Isn't it camp here, dears?" he said, as a small dog leapt upon him.

"I love the south specially," he went on. "I've got a small house in Agadir. You can have it any time you want. Just ask. You can swim nude with the boys and the seas are limpid."

Maybe this shows that by 1967 the gentlemen were starting to think about leaving Tangier, which had lost its special status, and going further south to places like Agadir.

It was sad that Joe and Kenneth H. didn't take Jimmy's advice and visit Agadir rather than returning to London – because, only a few weeks after Joe wrote the extract above and the next photo was taken, they met their tragic deaths.

Joe Orton (left) with the two Kenneths at the Windmill Café, May 1967

29
The Tangier Railway
by Paul Horler

The old railway winding around the beach in Tangier

Editor's introduction:
Expats often travelled between Tangier and Asilah for relaxation
(echoes of Agadir expats visiting Taghazout), a journey made very
easy for them in Tangier by the railway.

The train started from the port entrance, or sometimes even
inside the port, and made its way southwards to the port of Asilah.
From there the line went inland, so that the coastal town of Larache
just missed out on having a station. The line then headed towards
Fez, which the stories of Paul Bowles mention (e.g. "The Spider's
Web"), since he often travelled between Tangier and there.

Another rail branch went down to Marrakech, and several of
the gentlemen used to travel in both directions between Tangier and
Marrakech using the night train. Tim and Vincent remember how
pleasant it was, in their couchette from Marrakech – the last stage in
their journey from the deep south – to wake up early in the morning
and find themselves gliding gently along the beach in Tangier.

Yet Tangier's well-remembered railway along the beach had, as railways go, a surprisingly short life, and *Paul Horler* will now give us all the details.

Apart from a short railway along the old pier, which was itself pulled down in about 1930, the first railway along the seafront had been a narrow-gauge line built in about 1910 to help with building works.

Then in 1914, during the French protectorate, a railway company was formed to build a line from Fez to Tangier. But this was not completed until 1925, partly because of the war but afterwards because of problems going across the zones – it would have started in the French zone, gone into the Spanish and finished in the international zone. Even then it stopped well outside the city itself, at a location later renamed Tanger-Morara.

After quite a bit of discussion, the line was finally extended along the bay and the beach, up to the port entrance. The newly built white railway station, named Tanger-Ville, an elegant structure, was not opened until April 1934 – 25 years after the project had started!

There was also an extended track into the port area itself, along the breakwater, where eventually a third station, Tanger-Port, was built. During the insurrection, [31] the number of trains allowed into the International Zone was cut to three trains a week in 1955.

But by the 1970s there were five passenger trains a day along the beach, with one of these in the afternoon, starting from the port. Later in the day young locals used to love running along by the train and waving at trains as they trundled along the beach – and Rowan tells us it was not always just with their hands.

By then, however, the fact that beach users had to cross the line was felt to be a disadvantage. Not being able to get *off* the beach quickly enough because of the line was, for example, noted as a problem by some of our gentlemen friends, such as Stefan Rogers.

There was often an acute water shortage in Tangier, with lorries having to bring it in from the region of el Jadida, and so a water pipe was built alongside the railway, which added to the beach problems. All in all, the plan to take away the railway from the beach

---

[31] i.e. when the Moroccans were struggling for independence

and to widen the promenade did have advantages – for example the beach bars could be turned round to face the main Avenue Espagne.

The old station by the port finally closed in 2000, with the building becoming a police station and the terminus returning to the old, much less convenient, out-of-town location.

George Boreham was one of the elderly and respected expats who lived in Agadir[32], but he knew Tangier well and was scathing about the railway changes there: "They've closed down that lovely station in the centre," he told us, "and replaced it with an air-raid shelter two miles out of town!"

The gentlemen could no longer jump onto a train for a quick afternoon trip to Asilah, and they couldn't help thinking that another piece of old Tangier's essential atmosphere had gone forever.

*Last view of the old station (right), c. 1940,
with a steam train just visible by the platform*

---

[32] George Boreham, who has sadly now passed away, was one of the Agadir characters we will be telling you about, including the excellent work he did helping Moroccans, in our next proposed volume "Agadir to my Heart".

30
Caves of Hercules & Diplomatic Forest
by Tony Walton

Cafés near to the Caves of Hercules

The far north-west corner of Morocco is called Cape Spartel, about ten km west of Tangier. And four km south from the Cape are the Caves of Hercules.

The Rough Guide to Morocco has quite an illuminating comment on the caves: "Natural formations, occupied in prehistoric times, that are made the more striking by centuries of quarrying for millstones. There were still Moroccans cutting stone here for a living until the 1920s, but by that time their place was beginning to be taken over by professional guides and discreet sex hustlers." One assumes the hustlers were male rather than female!

However, activities there were often of an up-market nature too. During the 1920s, for instance, riding parties of the rich upper classes (mostly Spanish in those days) used to go there – ending with a picnic and champagne in the caves themselves.

In the 1950s, Cecil Beaton held a huge extravaganza there, where the guest were treated to champagne and hashish in a huge specially decorated cavern. Paul Bowles recorded, of the day: "Truman Capote, frightened of scorpions, had to be carried down the face of the cliff by a group of Moroccans to get there. An Andalucian orchestra was playing, surrounded by rocks and lanterns; the guests lay in moonlight among cushions on the sand."

Cafés almost inside the Caves of Hercules

The Diplomatic Forest was another small resort, on the way to the Caves of Hercules. It was called thus as the French ruling classes would have gone there for hunting purposes or 'to stick a pig.'

Horace Gendell, however, remembers that any taxi driver would take you out to the Foret Diplomatique to see the famous dancing boys. Almost magically, he recalls, a man with feathers in his hair and a coloured thobe (Arab dress) would play his drum, and dancing boys would come out of the forest, as if from nowhere, performing to the accompaniment of cymbals, drums and tin whistle. It was delightful to watch, and one enterprising friend of Horace's decided to import them all back to the Kasbah in Tangier once a week, to perform. The boys often wore bells around their ankles, loose fitting tunics and a hair band with flowers.

Tangier dancing boys became popular entertainment

Rupert Croft Cooke wrote a volume of his Tangier memoirs entitled "The Caves of Hercules," although curiously the Caves are hardly mentioned in it. Still, presumably he would have visited both the Caves and the Diplomatic Forest, as did also Barbara Hutton and most of the famous of Tangier when they needed a change of atmosphere. In fact, even more surprising, the restaurant near to the Caves on Robinson Beach, in the photo at the start of this chapter, was owned and developed by one of the king's female cousins.

In his diaries Joe Orton mentions a trip to the Diplomatic Forest, with his partner Kenneth Halliwell, but also with one of Tangier's rather notorious residents, George Greaves:–

George drove us to the Diplomatic Forest: "This is where to come if you want to get raped," he said....

...We passed through most beautiful countryside, the roads lined with mimosa and eucalyptus; blue mountains in the distance...

When we arrived at Asilah we stopped at the only tea place there, run by a Peter Churchill, a relative of the great man. An attractive teenage boy wearing nothing but a pair of red bathing trunks served us.

"That's Peter's boy," said George.

"So you'd better watch out!" Kenneth warned me.

As Joe Orton mentions George Greaves, and was fascinated by conversations with him, perhaps we could make a diversion to talk about this Tangier character. It was said that he could be the greatest friend but also a fearsome enemy! He was an Australian journalist whose knowledge of everyone's life made him a figure to be held in grudging respect, despite his rough and ready way of talking.

Michael Davidson wrote in his reminiscences that "to sit with George Greaves outside the Café de Paris or the Café Central was to become a privileged peeper into the souls of the passers-by...

"His eye would fall on a prosperous-looking Arab. 'That one,' he said, 'used to be the kept boy of a French minister. Now look at 'im – he wouldn't tell you the time if he 'ad two watches!'"

Rowan Tudor had heard about the Forest and went out there with a friend named Simon who claimed to be an expert on the place, although perhaps not quite as expert as George Greaves. Simon explained to him that they must both creep around silently in the long grass in the twilight, and would finally be sure to make contact with the desired object!

Rowan crept around in the grass silently and expectantly. After five minutes his hand met human flesh and a spasm of excitement went through him. His joy only lasted a few seconds – as it was Simon he had bumped into. After the same thing happened twice more, they returned to the Socco Chico for a nice cup of tea.

Paul Bowles was someone else who visited the Caves of Hercules occasionally – often accompanied by one of his proteges, Mrabet. Bowles also visited the Diplomatic Forest with another protege, Yacoubi, who was an artist of some standing. Paul was captivated both by his painting and by his love of animals, the latter being rather

Paul Bowles and Mohamed Mrabet at the Caves of Hercules

uncommon amongst Moroccans. All went well until Yacoubi took too much interest in a teenage German tourist and, when a complaint was made, neither the authorities nor Bowles were pleased...

Bowles' and Yacoubi's journalist companion to the Diplomatic Forest was named John Crosby, who wrote later about the visit in his New York column: "I was smitten by the infinitely seductive young dancers under the trees, until it dawned on me that they were boys, not girls. They were beautifully trained in the arts of dancing and homosexuality."

31

St Andrew's Church, Tangier

by Horace Gendell and Alan Moriarty

St Andrew's, the Church of England in Tangier, c.1925
"There is some corner of a foreign field, that is for ever England"

Horace recalls how St Andrew's Church itself was, and is, a beautiful little building and to this day well worth a visit. Visitors were still in 2003 being shown around St. Andrew's by a very polite Moroccan named Mustafa who had been there in the old days and who remembered many of the famous who had worshipped there – he loved talking to visitors about former times.

Editor:
Mustafa in 2003 drew my attention to a series of cartoons about life over the years at St Andrew's Church (see opposite).

The first shows how much religious toleration there was between the great faiths during the days of the International Zone – Muslim leaders are seen paying their respects at the funeral of Walter Harris, whom you will have read about earlier in this book. The second, less serious, shows poor Mustafa, on far right, coping with some tourists bursting in during a church service!

Horace:

One eccentricity, Horace recalls, was that the little church was in the diocese of 'Fulham and Gibraltar' – one can understand Gibraltar but wasn't Fulham rather a long way off?

In the 1960s Horace remembers how the church was a great meeting place for the expat gentlemen, almost like a social centre, and the padre during part of that era was not above getting involved in a few naughties himself. One of Horace's friends told him that once he went round to the vicar's house and stared in through the frosted glass; all he could make out was a pink bottom going up and down!

(*Ed.* How quickly, when talking about Tangier, can one move from the humorous to the very serious: because another source says that a vicar in the early 1970s committed suicide after he had been the subject of gossiping stories. Another indication of how the atmosphere in Tangier was changing in that decade.)

Alan Moriarty continues:

On my last visit to Morocco I spent only a short time in Tangier, but had time to visit the delightful Church of England, a great haven and meeting-place for expats. There I had the pleasure of meeting David Herbert – doyen of English expats.

Apart from David Herbert I also met the church organist, a grey-haired American quite inappropriately named Butch. He was a charming man, and the worst organist I have ever heard. But his movements at the console were exquisite; to see him pulling stops was a very poem – it was great if you put your fingers in your ears. After some chat, Butch took me aside and confided his problem (no, not that one – and no sniggering at the back, please).

It was approaching Easter, and he told me that he planned to put together a 'little choir' for the occasion. His problem, however, was that he had tenors and altos, but no basses. (No surprises there). Would I, he asked, sing bass in his little choir?

I said I would be delighted – lowering my speaking voice an octave or two.

But regrettably, mainly due to political events, it was not to be. And recently I learned that the church had been taken over by the evangelical holy rollers.

I am genuinely sad to think that time's ever-rolling stream has borne away Butch, his little choir, and their ilk.

David Herbert's grave, by the side of St Andrew's, Tangier

Other sources: Alec Waugh the author, mentioned elsewhere, said he was not religious but he attended St Andrew's to help him keep in touch with everyone: "In a small place like Tangier, I think you might back up the local parson, don't you agree?"

Woolman comments that he heard one reason why so many attended St Andrew's was 'to watch the ever-diverting spectacle of the silent feud between David Herbert and Robert Eliot, neither of whom could tolerate the other, possibly because they shared so much in common, yet who met every Sunday at St.Andrew's.'

The four things they had in common? First they were both church wardens at St. Andrew's; second they were both second sons of aristocratic parents, with the same background of Eton and Oxford (Eliot had been a page boy at King George VI's coronation in 1936); third they both possessed rambling villas on the Mountain, quite close to each other. And the fourth thing? – we will leave readers to work out .

It would be unfair, however, to take a too cynical view of attendance at St Andrew's. It did provide a place for British expats to meet each other on neutral ground. And St Andrew's, along with its catholic counterpart church, did a lot of useful work raising money for local charities. An annual fair was held to raise money for the Donkey Hospital and, more important, money was raised to support organisations like the Infant Welfare Centre which helped local Moroccans with sick children.

The 1940s was a time of great privation in Morocco as a whole (see Chapter 40, which mentions the dreadful poverty in the Rif area described in the book *For Bread Alone*). Although things were better in Tangier itself, many people came in from outside hoping to get help there. In addition to helping those poorer Moroccans, money was raised by Europeans in Tangier in the same epoch to help people who had fled from nearby Spain at the end of that very cruel civil war, including children of escapees.

Other countries in Europe had far too many problems of their own, both during and just after World War II, to worry about Spain, so a lot of useful charity work was done by comfortably-off Europeans in Tangier, and with St Andrew's and its wealthy congregation playing their part in co-ordinating it.

32
A Tangier fairy tale
by Fritz Heiner

My friend Albert in Agadir had a stable relationship with a youth named Mustapha, and everything was going for him (as you English say) swimmingly. Unfortunately, one year the local constabulary refused to renew his resident's permit. In my opinion it was because Albert had been indiscreet with Mustapha, whom he had taken openly into restaurants or hotels – acceptable in upmarket places like the Palais Salam in Taroudannt, but not in the ordinary ones.

In one sense it was a bad blow for him, but in another sense it was not so bad, as he had some property in Estepona in Spain.

The old city of Estepona in Andalucia, Spain

So Albert decided that he would go to live (for the second time) in Spain. And a few months later, I called in to see him at his new Estepona home, on my way from Germany to North Morocco through Malaga. He seemed very well settled and quite happy. The town of Estepona is very pleasant and is I think much less changed than some of the others along the Costa del Sol. We especially liked our visits to a restaurant named "Robbies" which had the most amazing décor. (I believe your English word is "camp"?)

Nevertheless there was something Albert was much missing. Yes, his young friend Mustapha.

Now while I stayed with him in his flat overlooking the bull-ring, he showed to me an advertisement which was in a special newspaper for English people living on the Costa del Sol.

The advertisement offered a tour of Tangier, with the coach collecting holiday-makers from their hotels or apartments along the Spanish coast and then, after two nights at the Hotel Cecil of Tangier, returning them to their bases in Spain.

Albert suggested that we went over there together... What clever plan was in his mind, I wondered?

The elegant Hotel Cecil in Tangier, between the wars

I discovered that Albert's plan (or pehaps your word is plot?) was that we were both to cross over from Algeciras to Tangier with the boat, but as a part of the large coach tour party. On arrival in Tangier I had to slip away to my favourite hotel, the Muniria, and then my room at the Hotel Cecil would be taken over by young Mustapha! Albert had telephoned to him in Agadir and persuaded him to come to Tangier with the bus.

I said to Albert that the whole thing brought to my mind that novel "The Wrong People", which was also set in Tangier, if you remember.

Of course this happened before everything was computerised, but even so we were surprised how smoothly everything went with our little plan. Albert and I arrived at the Hotel Cecil in Tangier, and then we went to sit outside the Café de Paris, where we had agreed to meet young Mustapha.

Albert was still worried that he would not arrive from Agadir. But we had taken only one coffee when Mustapha walked up to our table, smiling and looking radiant.

Since it was a large coach party, no one in the Hotel Cecil noticed that the guest in Room 113 had been changed from me into a glamorous young man.

It also reminded me a little of one of our German fairy tales, in which the old woman is transformed into a beautiful maiden!

Well you know, I am not sure how things continued after Albert and Mustapha's joyful re-union, although we all succeeded in having one evening meal together (near Tangier port, and a safe distance from *both* the hotels) before I departed to Asilah as planned.

I am not certain if Albert smuggled Mustapha back to Spain in the coach party, and I preferred not to ask. I heard later that he had set up a holiday base for the two of them on the coast of Morocco near to Kenitra, because there was nothing to stop Albert from going there on his holidays, while at the same time keeping his permanent base in Spain.

But I somehow feel they stayed together in one of the two countries, even though I lost my contact with them. We want to hope (as they say at the end of our German fairy tales) that "wenn sie nicht gestorben sind, leben sie noch heute."

I believe your usual English translation is: "they lived happily ever after," but another translation could be: "if they have not died, they are still together today."

> *Editor:* Fritz Heiner wrote this story some time ago. Since then Albert has passed away, but rumour has it that he and Mustapha did manage to link up together in Spain and also found a holiday home for a while by Kenitra Beach in Morocco.

A view of Kenitra Beach in Morocco.[33]

---

[33] Kenitra Beach had become important in World War II as it saw the first American landings this side of the Atlantic.

33

Crossing the Straits by *Alan Moriarty*

On my last-ever visit to Tangier I crossed the Strait of Gibraltar – though not for the first time – in extraordinary circumstances. A French sailing friend of mine, Luc, was intending to travel to Morocco and round the coast of North Africa with a young crew; and he asked for my help to cross the Strait. We set out, inadvisably perhaps, on the morning of New Year's Day, after prolonged greeting of Hogmanay – which Gibraltar knows how to celebrate as well as anywhere, being full of Scotsmen, most of them soldiers.

At first the crossing went well. But the weather quickly deteriorated – also, Luc had recently made a new friend, and soon both were enthusiastically engaged with each other in the forward cabin, leaving me on deck wrestling with the wheel.

The Strait of Gibraltar is a fearsome place in January; a gale howled in the rigging, the waves were high, steep, and curling over the decks, and now I could see the line of foam where surf broke at the foot of the Atlas Mountains. The yacht was huge and metal-hulled; I could make little impression on the steering, and it seemed clear that we were about to be dashed to perdition on the rocks. I banged on the hatch, and Luc appeared, slightly dishevelled.

"Oui?"

"I need some help up here."

Luc's head revolved briefly, then he shrugged. "You are doing very vell." And he disappeared. Clearly he was a true Frenchman, in that nothing mattered in comparison with *l'amour*.

But all was not lost. Luc's head reappeared. "You should only vurry," he said, "ven you can smell the camel-shit."

Having delivered this gem of counsel, he submerged permanently, or at least until we got into Tangier, which was managed somehow or other. Here, though, Luc showed his true mettle. Faced with a truculent and bureaucratic immigration officer, he asked, "You have a glass?"

Luc produced a litre bottle of Chivas Regal, obtained in Gibraltar, and filled the customhouse mug to the brim. Magically, our documents were stamped within a few moments, and we were in.

Later that night, though, there was a banging on the hatch; it was the immigration officer again, accompanied by two grim-faced colleagues. Woops! How long do they give you for attempted bribery of officials?

"Oui?"

"Do you haf any more of that visky?"

Fortunately we had, and it was again smiles all round. Some things, at least, don't change. But Luc's adventure ended unhappily. From the Moroccan coast he sailed across the Atlantic and, once in the USA, his crew deserted, so that – at stupefying expense – he had to have his yacht shipped back to France in a huge wooden crate. *Quel horreur*.

Back in Tangier, I parted from Luc, and my contact with Morocco was minimal this time. I walked across the port, which felt like any other busy docks, caught the ferry to Algeciras, and – like the British regiments then leaving the Rock for ever – I returned to England from Gibraltar for the last time.

Tangier harbour – a frequent exit point

PART THREE:
IN THE TANGIER REGION

34
Meanwhile in Gibraltar
by Jim Tate

Editor: Gibraltar, as you know, is a UK dependency just over the water from Tangier, with frequent ferries between the two.

Often expats in Tangier would visit Gib for the British banks and so on. But, as this extract shows, it was very much a holiday destination in its own right. Jim Tate now provides us with some memories of a holiday he once had there.

In the summer of 1969 I was 21 and my friend Steve was 18. I had lodged with Steve while I was at university. We had become sort of lovers but in an innocent sort of way. Other than the friendship between each other, neither of us had any other gay experience, never having been to a gay (called queer in those days) pub or club; neither had we ever visited cottages. There were almost no university gay societies, gay groups or gay press at that time.

For some reason we decided to go on a holiday to Gibraltar, which entailed staying at a hotel there for one week.

We soon discovered by talking to other guests in the hotel bar that the main British military in Gibraltar were RAF personnel. One woman guest we spoke to on the first night was very keen to get me into bed with her. Steve and I were very careful to appear to be straight, as we thought it would be dangerous to be blatantly gay – we, of course, had always been like that, as it certainly would have been dangerous (and from the police) to be seen to be gay. She did not get me into bed, by the way, and it was from another guest in the hotel that we learnt on the last day of the holiday that the woman was in fact a transvestite – he had had sex with 'her'.

A British airman visiting the hotel bar told us about another bar that was along a road by the harbour, running along the bottom face of a cliff. Also that the bar was built into a cave in the cliff and that it was the liveliest bar in Gibraltar. So Steve and I paid it a visit. We sat at a table drinking a beer, when a much older man came to sit opposite us. We got chatting and he insisted on buying us both gin and tonics (large). When we had finished, we offered to buy him a drink, but he refused and got up and bought us two more g& t's.

He repeated this for some time even though we tried to stop him without offending him, but he was very insistent, especially as he also was drinking as much as us both, if not more. It occurred to me that he was trying to get us drunk, so I nudged Steve and whispered to him that we should pour our drinks on the floor from under the table when he wasn't looking, which we did. After several more drinks there was a large amount on liquid flowing out from under our table – and we thought that it was time to exit.

So as an excuse Steve and I got up to go to the loo, which was at the back of the bar. As the light in the bar was a bit dim we hadn't noticed that there was an open doorway at the back. We had a look in there out of curiosity and saw that it was an inner bar with no windows and was even more dimly lit than the first bar. Also, unlike the first bar, there were only men present, some of them clearly very much together!

It was the first time Steve and I had been in what was obviously a gay bar, but we soon felt very much at home. It wasn't long before we had joined a group of other gays in there, who all seemed to be very friendly. Some of them seemed to be British airmen, and some seemed to be Gibraltarians. But, as far as we could tell, none of them were rent boys.

After a while we noticed yet another door at the back of this bar! Our new-found friends suggested that we have a look in there, which we did, even though by this time we had become a little inebriated. The door led into yet another room that was pitch black and where almost immediately Steve and I got involved in sexual activities with other men. It was our first experience of a dark room.

The Rock, as seen from La Linea in Spain

During the week, Steve and I had many sexual encounters with local men, Spanish, German – and British airmen but oddly enough no sailors. Their ages ranged from 16 to 50. Many of them we met in the bar in the cliff, or through their friends. We only met one gay person at the hotel, but we didn't get involved with him. We didn't hear of, or go to, any cottages – although I suppose there must have been some. Nor did we meet any Arab people there.

We did, however, have a day trip to Tangier – during which we were accosted many times by Arab young men who were offering anything. When we rather incautiously mentioned that we were gay (by that time we had become somewhat bold), they offered their private company for less than the price of a beer in the UK. I am afraid that we weren't bold enough to avail ourselves of their offers. Fortunately, it was all done in good natured fashion.

By the end of the week both Steve and I had learnt a lot about gay life, and we were not quite so naïve as at the beginning.

35
The Fifties on the Spanish Costas
by Peter Middlegate and others

Editor: Still on the subject of coastal resorts, neighbouring Spain used to have things in common with old Tangier. So here are some memories of the Costas Spain in the middle Franco years (the late 1950s) when the country was first being opened up to tourists. We will then tell you about the large number of Spanish in Tangier.

Peter Middlegate: My distant memory is that the young Spanish guys in the 1950s were enthusiastic for contact and friendship with the single English tourists on the Costa Brava and Costa del Sol. But the Spanish police did everything they could to prevent it, short of stopping the tourists from coming – they were desperate for our currency in those days.

The young Spaniards, just like in Morocco round the same time, were members of big families and could get hold of some much-wanted money in this way, a lot of which found its way back home. Nowadays big families in Spain are a rarity, although you still get them in Morocco I think.

But was it just the money and the poverty? Do you know I wonder if there was another factor which 1950s Spain, and Morocco not so long ago, had in common? In Spain the virginity of the girls was considered terribly important during the Franco years, to the extent that boys were hardly allowed near the girls. It was as hard-line as the Muslim attitude – anyone who tried to violate the girls' virginity could be in very serious trouble indeed.

It sort of created a kind of wild randy-ness amongst the young men, gathering together in large numbers without any female moderating social influence or even company, where they just wanted to have some fun and prove how virile they were. At the same time they knew that the (nearly always older) gay man would treat them kindly and would offer them friendship. I think youths in large families can often be very lonely and need someone to make them feel special and "wanted."

Nowadays of course Spanish couples have only a small number of children and that makes a big difference. The modern *average* Spanish straight youth (obviously some are gay) wouldn't dream of going with tourists for gay sex in return for gifts because he is 100% girl-orientated, socially as well as sexually, even if he could still be a bit short of money. But in those days, yes, he might well go with gays. Any feelings of guilt? Well, he passed that on to the gay man, I suppose.

Sitges in Spain

Very much to back up what Peter says above, another friend recalls how Sitges, the famous gay resort in Catalonian Spain, started the ball rolling in the 1950s by being a place where English gentlemen went to meet young Spanish fishermen, rather than to meet each other! Only later did it become a place for conventional gays.

No doubt mainstream gays, who go out there for the pub and club scene in Sitges nowadays, would be surprised to discover how it had all started, and again it would be very unusual for modern Spanish fishermen etc. etc. to get involved in such things.

Before and after, on the Costas. How life must have changed there.

The Spanish in Tangier

Why are we returning (briefly) to Tangier City in the middle of this Spanish chapter? Well, at the beginning of the twentieth century the Spanish regarded Tangier as their own city and Spanish influence there was very strong indeed. Most of the city outside the ancient Medina was built by the Spanish – as the next photo bears witness.

So having read Peter Middlegate's account of life on the Costas Spain, it will make more sense of what follows.

The Spanish theatre in Tangier, built 1913

Ron Nelson told me that back in the 1950s Tangier was full of young Spanish trying to escape from the poverty of Franco's Spain and frequenting the various bars looking for a financial backer. As Spain became more prosperous the situation did indeed radically change, but in those days, Ron recollected, bars often had upstairs rooms where one could get to know the young Spanish better, although he never took advantage of such facilities himself!

It seems so strange to us from a 21st century perspective to think of young Spaniards going to Morocco to seek their fortune, but there really was a lot of poverty in Spain prior to their tourist boom of the 1960s, as Peter Middlegate's account earlier in this chapter testifies. Tangier on the other hand had one of its slightly more prosperous periods in the late 1950s – plus the fact that the police of old Tangier were less stringent than the Spanish police under Franco.

Of course by the *end* of the twentieth century the situation had completely reversed itself. An interesting book by Tahar Ben Jalloun called "Leaving Tangier" describes how young Tanjawis in the 1980s longed to escape and get to Spain.

36
Trips to Asilah
by Horace Gendell and Alan Moriarty

Editor's note:
Asilah and Larache had been in the old Spanish zone of Morocco, which was in the north of the country and about the size of Belgium (whereas the French zone, taking up the rest of Morocco, was about the size of France).

The Spanish Zone had developed a different culture to the main part, with Tetuan as its capital and Spanish as its second language after Arabic. It virtually surrounded Tangier, and so even a short trip out of the International Zone of Tangier usually meant you were going into the Spanish zone.

Horace starts:
Sometimes I would travel the fifteen mile journey south from Tangier along the coast to the delightful seaside port and resort of Asilah, where another small colony of expats lived. The railway ran between the two. (I am told that in a similar way, the gentlemen in Agadir would visit the coastal village of Taghazout, where things would often be calmer than in the main city.)

In Asilah we Tangier gentlemen did indeed find the atmosphere less commercial and more relaxing, as did also Peter Churchill,[34] a distant relation of the great leader, who lived there permanently.

Now there were three beaches in Asilah then – the north one wide open and spacious down towards the railway station, another smaller one near the charming fishing port and a third one, picturesque and rocky, on the southern side – with the colourful Medina (probably the prettiest in Morocco) between the second and third beaches. At the southern tip of the medina was a spit sticking out into the sea almost like a pier and called the Craciche, which was I think quite a good meeting place.

---

[34] Rupert Croft-Cooke was apparently amused by the title of Peter's autobiography ' All My Sins Remembered'

Peter Churchill had a house near there overlooking the more secluded rocky beach, and I remember it being almost like Paradise – both very beautiful and with an easy availabilty of charming locals for friendship. When I visited him it was wonderful for me just to sit on his balcony, taking the view in and wondering if I could ever find anywhere more perfect.

Asilah's medina and port: photo taken from the Craciche jetty, which was itself a meeting place.

Alan Moriarty continues:
My first trip to Morocco was in the 1960s when I was a wide-eyed and moderately green student on one of my first trips abroad. I was on a 'safari holiday'. To explain: small settlements of native-type huts with conical straw roofs had been established throughout the country, and the 'safari' consisted simply of being conveyed in a battered bus from one such settlement to another, spending several days in each.

But hey, it was cheap, we were all young, and most of us – probably all of us – were on our first trip to the African continent.

Our main base was near the then-delightful seaside town of Asilah, not far south from Tangier. The location was magical, the sort of place you dream about in a foggy English winter – long palm-lined beaches fringing the dark blue Atlantic, and wonderful, warm sunshine. The village itself was a small fishing settlement with clusters of tiny coloured cottages, and a lazy, relaxed air about it. Just outside the village, a multitude of rocks tumbled down to the sea on either side.

In the afternoons and on holidays these rocks were alive with enthusiastic young fishermen, plying long poles, though never with visible success. They were friendly, I found – in fact, very friendly indeed.

I was always approached at once, and the opening gambit was invariably, "Gotta cigarette?" Though not a smoker, I quickly learned to carry a plentiful supply. Also I learned that the better type of English cigarettes were especially welcome. Every afternoon I met the charming Laroussie; he didn't smoke either, simply tucked the cigarettes I gave him into his tee-shirt pocket, doubtless to sell later. It was a small price to pay for an hour or so of pleasant dalliance among the rocks – and it was also in Asilah that a friend of Laroussie introduced me to 'kif'.

I obtained, as recommended, in a café, the traditional pipe with small bowl and long stem. I puffed away, feeling very daring – but the stuff did nothing for me, either then or on subsequent trials; all I got was a sore throat and runny nose. Tant pis.

On my final trip to Tangier some years later I simply had to revisit Asilah but it was a big disappointment. The old village had gone, so had the rocks and the young fishers; now it was a medium-sized industrial seaport, with a concrete expanse of docks and grey buildings in place of one of the beaches. I spent half a day and a night there, but nobody spoke, nobody smiled. I left, again sad at heart.

Eheu fugaces! Where now were Laroussie and his friends?

On next page are last views of Asilah Medina:
parts that have changed little over the years.

Outside and inside Asilah's Medina

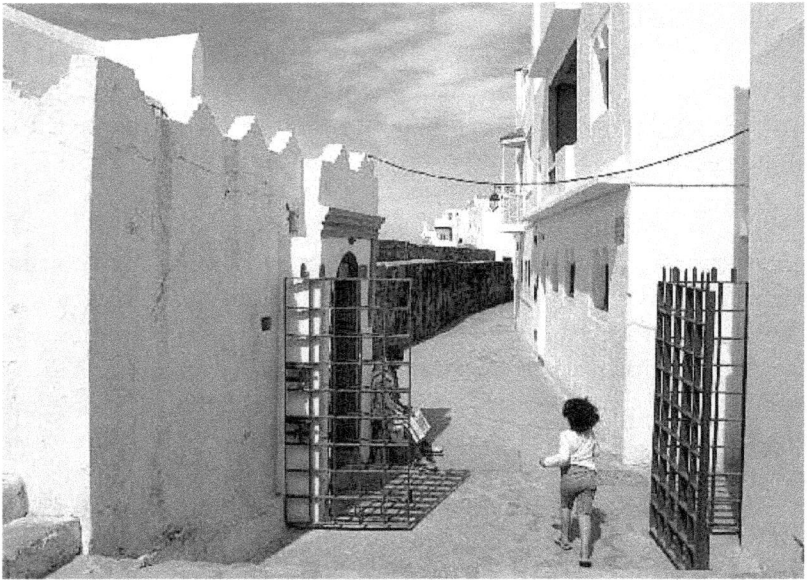

37
Fez street life
Contributed by Adrian Hammond

Introduction by the editor:

Fez is very much in the northern region of Morocco, fairly easy to reach from Tangier by rail.

It was the ancient capital of the Marghreb, an area larger than what we now call Morocco. There was also a historic link with Tunisia, in that a group of refugees fled from the other very ancient city of North Africa, Kairouan, and settled in Fez – founding one of the first universities in the western hemisphere, which they called the Kairouan. Later on, some other refugees from another long-established Muslim city, Cordoba in Spain, also came to Fez.

Perhaps its welcoming nature has made Fez more tolerant of homosexuality over the centuries than some other Moroccan cities. According to the Encylopaedia of Homosexuality, in past centuries the Fez bath-houses "were the subject of scandalous comments."

General Lyautey, the liberal French governor of Morocco, was careful not to destroy any of the ancient areas of Fez with modernisation, and his decision to build a new city (Ville Nouvelle) to the south west of the two old ones meant it was relatively easy for some gay activities to go on within that new city but without offending the most traditional elements.

Paul Bowles often visited there during his long years in Tangier. One of his easier to read novels, "The Spider's Web", is set there during the days of the struggle for independence and is considered one of the great political thrillers.

Bowles used to say that Fez was the odd-man-out amongst Moroccan cities: "The visitor feels something in (Old) Fez which he describes as a feeling of mystery... the city seems inexhaustible, complex, and vaguely menacing...many visitors have a negative reaction to its twisting alleys, teeming with people and animals ...to grasp the fascination of the place one has to enjoy being lost in a crowd and being pushed along, not caring where to or for how long...Fassis feel intuitively that everything must be hidden."

Fez street musicians

In 1979 some French journalists investigated the lives of Fez's younger citizens. They carried out a series of interviews spoken into a tape recorder. These were later all written up in French in detail, but have never appeared in English. *Adrian Hammond* has, however, very kindly translated one of the several interviews for us, and it is an interesting record. So over to Adrian now:–

This interview I am translating is perhaps the most revealing and significant in the book on the subject of friendship between the races.
The words of the interviewer are in italics. The interviewee starts by introducing himself.

The lads call me Bidos. I live in the Rcif district.
Do all your family live in Fez?
Yes, in the Rcif district. My father works in France, my mother in the house – she is a Berber and makes kaftans – clothes. She does not sell them – she takes them to the merchants.

Do you have brothers and sisters?
Yes, seven, 4 brothers and 3 sisters. One brother is a guide like me.

Where did you learn French?
At school and also from tourists.

So you want to make this guiding work, your "metier" (French word meaning trade or profession).
Yes but I hope also to get enough money to go to France and learn another "metier".

Did you start your work as a guide when you were still at school?
Yes, in my last year I did two hours after school each day.

Boujeloud Gardens, near to which this interview took place

How do you make contact with your customers?
I just see a tourist and ask him if he would like a guide – if he is interested in having a student he says "okay!"

And what do you suggest to him?
(Bido then lists all the famous sites in Fez he could take him to visit. He also mentions the "panorama view," which is genuine and very

splendid, but one must add that to get to the finest viewpoints the tourist would need be taken up to lonely, shrub-covered spots up on the hills – so there could well have been a discreet second purpose.)

You tell them you are a student?
Yes, they like students very much. *(he laughs)*

You take him also to the people selling things?
Oh yes, I take the tourists to see the merchants. First of all to the one selling leather goods and if they buy I get twenty per cent. Then I take them to the carpet merchants and if they buy I get a commission of fifteen or twenty per cent. That's our way of life.

How much do you charge the tourist?
If he is quite happy he will pay well. If he is not happy he pays what he wants. But making their acquaintance *(the French word is connaissance)* is more important to me.

What do you mean by connaissance?
How shall I put it? – getting to know people. Afterwards lots of people write to me.

But when I first met you, you suggested we visited the Medina and I said I already knew it. Didn't you propose something else to me?
I asked you if you wanted to be alone with me. If you had said Yes we would have done it straightaway, or at the end of the tour – if not, then I would have said goodbye.

You ask all tourists at the end of the tour if they want to be alone with you?
Well not always. I watch their eyes. I know people – I watch them carefully. If they smile and laugh I know that's what they want.

.When a tourist agrees – that he is okay to be alone with you – what happens and where do you go?
Oh maybe I lead him into the Borj Sud – countryside round here. No, at first I ask him how much he will give me. If the price pleases me, then okay. If not then I say No.

And what would the tourist do then, if you say No?
Maybe he goes to find another guide.

Okay, so you agree the price go into the countryside and what happens?
Oh you know – but it never takes more than half an hour.

Are there tourists who prefer other things ?
Tell me what you mean. You can say the word.

They might prefer to suck you for example.
(He smiles) Oh yes, that would be very fine!

And they might want to f - - - you?
 (He laughs) Oh no, monsieur, no. That's something else! That never, never! I am not a whore. If he wants a whore he can go to Pigalle (a district of Paris). I am a man with a zizi.

Do you sometimes see the same tourist again?
Yes, often over several months.

What sort of tourists?
Normally French. Well, once with an American who gave me 500 dirhams (this would have been about £30). Also other French speakers who come to Fez – like Canadians.

Would you sometimes spend the night with him?
Yes, if he pays me well and I like him.

Where would you go to spend the night?
To a hotel. I leave my card at reception. *(Moroccans over 17 have an identity card).* And I spend all the night in the hotel and they don't ask me questions. He pays well for the whole night.

Do you sometimes go on a trip with a tourist?
Yes if he has a hired car or a car from France. One week, two weeks or three months. If he pays well, maybe for all my life.

Do you make more by going with men than actually being a guide?
Yes I do.

How much do you yourself make in a week?
It could be nothing at all except a packet of cigarettes, or another week maybe 1000 dirhams (£60) or even 2000.

What do you do with the money?
Clothes, cigarettes, cinema – and I give some to my mother, because my father is in France.

Does your mother know what you do?
She knows I am a guide but does not know about the other thing. If she found out I would have to leave the house. She does not live very close to here (the tourist area), luckily.

And how do the people of Fez see all this?
They know about it and they make a joke about it .They say 'Oh you are going with a man, you are going to "casser avec lui la cacahuete?

What do you mean by "casser la cacahuete"?
Breaking open the peanut – it means you are going to give it to him up the – after you have taken him out into the countryside.

There is some open countryside very close to the city of Fez

The people make fun of you?
No. They just smile and say "Ah, you are going to casser la cacahuete and going into the countryside." They notice but do not say much

You go with girls?
No, I am saving myself. I cannot go with them. I do not want to yet.
We are not allowed to make love with Moroccan girls..

Lake with swimmers in Boujeloud Gardens, near scene of the interview

Final comment by Adrian:
One could add, on the subject of love-making, that the fact that these
young Moroccan guys from Fez, and presumably others like them in
other Moroccan towns, refused to indulge in <u>passive</u> gay intercourse
(others also emphasised strongly their refusal several times in the
other Fez interviews) may well have helped stop the AIDS virus
spreading into Morocco during the 1980s.

38
Fez: the ones you just miss
by John Hoopard

Guides waiting at Bab Boujeloud, c. 1985

A friend of mine, Ralph, used to say "The ones that you just miss are the ones that you most remember". I never knew quite what he meant until I visited Fez back in about 1985.

I stayed initially at the Hotel Rex in Ville Nouvelle. I want to pay a tribute to this type of Moroccan hotel because they used to be such good value, costing a few pounds a night, with obliging staff, clean sheets changed frequently and with the usual hand basin and comfy bed in a quiet room. At the Rex there was even a nice, friendly little café downstairs where you could have breakfast.

The young Moroccans whom I saw in Fez were not kids and seemed very nice. One of the details I liked about them was that many of them wore shorts, which was very sensible with the heat, but it was the only Moroccan city I came across where this was the custom. A friend had said a good café to meet them was the Café de la Résistance in Ville Nouvelle. ("Not much resisitance there!" he said, and he was right.) There they made it clear they were available for friendship – but I had no idea where we could go to be private.

In addition, Fez has, bewilderingly, four separate townships – in order of age: el Bali, el Jadid, Ville Nouvelle, Nouvelle Medina.

The oldest part of Fez, el Bali, is a labyrinth of ancient streets, but it's a working city too – probably the oldest working city in the world.

Each of the four townships seemed to be separated from the next by about a five minute bus journey or a fifteen minute walk. In this confusing panorama, eventually I found a sympathetic middle-aged guide who was willing to take me under his protection. It wasn't long before I confided in him that I needed sympathetic accommodation too – so should I be fortunate enough to meet an agreeable, in both senses, companion I would at least be prepared.

He advised me that the best accommodation for me would be in the form of the Hotel des Jardins, situated under the walls of the very attractive Fez el Jadid, and I took his advice. (By the way Fez el Jadid means literally New Fez but it was built in the 13th century, whereas Fez el Bali was built in the 11th!).

So I now had two rooms – one in Ville Nouvelle at the Rex Hotel, where I had left my passport and valuables, and another three or four miles away in Fez el Jadid where I had left nothing more valuable than water and a few personal items.

Getting from one part of Fez to another involved a lot of walking

I have to say that, on the surface at least, the Hotel des Jardins was a very "low life" establishment and to be honest I was nervous of staying there, although my view quickly changed..

The bedrooms were set out around an oblong gallery from which one could look into the courtyard below. To my initial alarm, I found that the hotel had a policeman in the room opposite – no problem at all I discovered, and he seemed very friendly. In the next room to me there was the most charming family, consisting of father, mother and three young children, all in one room and all of whom seemed to take an instant liking to me, and I to them. I was only too pleased to give the family (always through the father) any little treats I could find, and I was beginning to feel like an American arriving in Europe at the end of World War Two.

I slept the first night surprisingly well and the next morning woke bright and early, seeing the sun rising over the gorgeous walls of Fez el Jadid. I decided to go and explore the new vicinity, being struck by how friendly all the locals were – no doubt puzzled why this foreign gentleman had *not* ensconced himself in one of the luxury hotels a mile or two away, but too polite to ask questions.

The shops were little booths in odd corners of the walls between Babs – in fact the whole of this part of Fez seemed to consist of nothing but walls and Babs. 'Babs', as you probably know, are large and sometimes dramatic gateways into the walls, and there must be about a thirty of them, if not more, in Fez.

Photo by Alan Moriarty.

Leaving the hotel I arrived under a different Bab – where I beheld an apparition sent from heaven… Sitting under the gateway was the original all-American college boy, extremely handsome, rosy cheeked, fair-haired with a crew cut, Doc Martin boots and not the usual shorts but corduroy long trousers. Just how could this wonderful slice of American pie have found his way into Fez?

I might just mention that there seemed to be a large bulge in his brown corduroys, which could have been explained ten years later with the advent of those chunky mobiles we had in the 1990s, but they hadn't yet been invented.

I asked him if he was 'Americain' and he replied "Non", smiling – as if he was always being asked the same question and ready for yet another round of the usual guessing game.

"Allemand?"... "Non." "Espanol?"... "Non."

Puzzling...clearly time to give up, even though he was enjoying it all, so I asked him point blank where he was from.

"Le Maroc!" he replied triumphantly and with a huge grin.

I decided not to ask indiscreet questions about his father, but suggested he should come and have a break in my place at the nearby Hotel des Jardins, where he could tell me the story of his life.

Yes, yes he would really love to, truly – but "A little later!" Did that bulge get bigger when I suggested coming back? He explained to me he was a tour guide (no doubt unofficial) and was expecting a good crowd of tourists to arrive very soon.

We went on chatting and finally I persuaded him that, as there was no sign of the tourists turning up, he should come up to my room for coffee. He jumped up quickly with another huge grin and, with something else definitely jumping up for joy his corduroys, we started walking towards the hotel... In the distance I could now see the front hall and I waved to the helpful guardian on the door, who waved back to me in a friendly, knowing way.

Nearly there, nearly there...Within five yards of us reaching the door, there was a sudden "jabber, jabber, jabber" on the street from the right and – yes – the tourists were at last arriving!

"Spater," the lovely youth said to me, using the German word for "later", and quickly marched over to greet them, after giving me a very sweet but apologetic smile and shrug.

Yes, he would have been very popular with the tourists.

Needless to say I never saw him again. I stayed in Fez for quite a bit longer but I just couldn't forget the all-American dream, and maybe searching for him stopped me forming friendships with others.

To add insult to injury, at my favourite Fez café, the Zanzibar, they played one record over and over again: "Bye, bye, American pie."

Café Zanzibar in Fez's Ville Nouvelle

Yet oddly enough it was at Café Zanzibar that at the very end of the holiday, after I'd given up hope of findng American Pie, I met a really lovely couple of shoe-shiners whom I took to straightaway. (I think there was some system in those days of a youngish shoe shiner going round with an older one, as a kind of apprenticeship).

But it was on my *last day*, after I'd given up my room at the Hotel des Jardins and when I was ready to go home. Both of them could not have been nicer, but it was much too late to do anything beyond having a very mild dalliance.

So for the second time, it was the ones I just missed who are the ones now that I most remember.

39

My two trips to Fez

by Alan M oriarty

1968. Travelling from Tangier on a group excursion, this was my first visit to Fez, the ancient capital of Morocco.

As soon as our coach bus arrived in the main station we were met by an enthusiastic reception committee. Most were selling souvenirs, as always (very good, very cheap), but I was fascinated to see that other merchandise was widely available. "You come with me, I give you good time" – and one of the eager deputation, so that there would be no misunderstanding, poked his finger in his open mouth, jerking it in and out; another tapped his rear. I found myself, not for the first time, in the excruciatingly difficult position that, as a member of a group, I didn't dare show any interest.

One of the young unwashed, regrettably frustrated in his advances to me, pointed to another member of our group, who happened to be wearing bright pink trousers. "Look at his trousers! He'll be interested!" he said. But he wasn't.

For the moment, we moved on. But I hadn't come all the way to Morocco to pass up such a chance to experience the local culture at first hand.

The next day, as I recall, the group went on a guided tour; I detached myself and went on my own tour, starting at the bus station.

Initially I was disappointed, as the welcoming group clearly homed in on arriving buses, especially those carrying tourists. But soon I found Abdul, slim and eager, who offered himself as a guide. This was a start, and we set off – though I didn't take in very much, as I was wondering how to broach the topic that had been so delicately raised yesterday. I was very young.

The tour was coming to an end when, clutching at conversational straws I asked, "How much money do you make at this?" He said, "Not so much. Most in the summer, when English poofs come." He looked at me sideways, "Are you a poof, mister?"

I gulped, then asked, "Where can we go?"

"The swimming-pool. We share a cubicle, we swim, then we go in the cubicle again."

Of course. But on the way to the pool my attention was diverted by an amazingly beautiful young Berber; he was clear-skinned, only lightly tanned, after his race, and – very unusually –- flowing blond hair tumbled almost to his shoulders. He wore a scarlet shirt and ragged green pants. Brown, dirty ankles poked out underneath, with leather sandals on sockless feet.

Abdul, who missed nothing, asked, "You want him?" He stopped his friend, called Abdou-Raschi, and a whispered conversation followed. Again a bargain was struck, and I arrived at the pool with my two companions, worrying about what the attendant would think of a white European who wanted to share a cubicle with two young Moroccans. But he hardly looked up.

I can hardly pretend that our fumblings in the tiny cubicle represented one of the great encounters of history, but it was nonetheless an experience, much enjoyed I think by all, made more memorable still by the abrupt entrance of a huge and hairy rat that ran across my feet before disappearing again, almost as soon as I had noticed it. My companions seemed to think it was nothing unusual.

As I said, an experience.

Between the two oldest cities in Fez.

1991. My second trip to Fez began unpromisingly.

Immediately I arrived in the suburbs in my hired car I was surrounded by unprepossessing youths on mopeds who followed me like a swarm of hornets (and equally welcome), constantly banging on my windows every time I stopped. Repeatedly I thought that, by ducking round side-streets, I could avoid them but, at the next intersection, there they would be again! It had become a nightmare. I wanted to find a hotel where I would be in some degree isolated from this brigade, but on the other hand I didn't want them to see where I was staying. As a last resort I drove well out of town, leaving them behind, and returned by a completely different route.

This time I was lucky.

Once settled into a hotel I went into the centre of town and was approached almost immediately. "You want -- --?"

He looked nice; I didn't know quite what I wanted, but was willing to go where the adventure led. I raised the usual difficulty. "I've nowhere to go, though."

That was no problem. "Come with me."

There is a wide park[35] near the centre of Fez and my new friend, Hassim, led the way towards a thick cluster of bushes. But I became uneasy. As always, the town centre was full of idlers, and, as we crossed to the park, every eye in town had seemed to follow us. I also reflected that I was carrying my passport, credit cards and all my money. Things would probably be okay, but...it would just be too big a risk. In a rare moment of common sense, I made an assignment to meet Hassim that evening, after dark.

I didn't expect Hassim to turn up, but he did, dead on time. Again, there was the problem of where to go, and I certainly wasn't going back to the bushes again. There was only one solution... The back of a small hired car, even when parked in the countryside, is no place for amatory gymnastics – but, still, it was fun for both of us, and we parted on excellent terms.

Next day, things seemed to be going even better. At the edge of the Medina, I was asked if I wanted a guide. My questioner was extremely easy on the eye – also, I found it was always an excellent idea to attach oneself to a semi-permanent guide as it kept the others

[35] photos of Boujeloud Gardens on page 201 and 205

away. For some reason (I forget what) he couldn't come with me that day, so we arranged to meet the following morning. I was unsure just what would be on offer, but was prepared to wait.

Back in the hotel, however, disturbing news awaited me. As soon as I went in, a grim-faced manager approached, and said that he advised me to leave as soon as possible.

"Leave the hotel?"
"No, leave Morocco!"
Good Lord, how had they found me out so quickly? But the reality was more complex. In the big world outside, Kuwait had recently been invaded by Iraq, and the Americans, a few hours ago, had started firing missiles at Iraqi installations. There was great anger in the Muslim world and, as always in the Muslim mind, Americans and British were inseparable. I could be at serious risk, I was told.

In fact, I was never at any real risk – but at the time it looked like Armageddon might be upon us, and my main worry was that transport communications could be cut off. Already panic-stricken Americans were leaving by the bus-load.

I decided to leave next morning, but first I met my new friend to explain. He was puzzled and disappointed, but a little conciliatory gift, as ever, made all the difference.

I got the Algeciras ferry and caught a flight back to London from Gibraltar. A great pity.

40

Jean Genet and the expats of Larache

by Tony Walton (with a section of memories by others).

The number of authors who lived in and wrote about Tangier is huge. Yet I was surprised to discover that, not so far away, there is *almost* a rival town to Tangier for the number of literary folk who have lived there.

Larache, set like Tangier in the northern region of Morocco and not too far from its own sister town of Asilah, does seem to have been a visiting place for some of the expat gentlemen [36], but my main aim is to talk about the expat writers who have lived, or returned there, including France's most famous gay author, Jean Genet.

The north end of Larache's "Atlantic Balcony" with the fortress dominating it from an even higher point

Larache is built near the ancient Roman city of Lixus (site of one of the Labours of Hercules – the golden apples in the Garden of the Hesperides).

---

[36] Paul Okken, Rowan and Tim give us some memories halfway through this section.

The town also has one of the most spectacular seafronts in Morocco. The high promenade, with justification, is called the "Atlantic Balcony", high up above the sea with the old fort up high and with a rocky, rugged coastline down below, reminiscent of the Malacom in Havana.. Wonderful views stretch along the coast in both directions, including the beach over on the other side of the river estuary.

What Larache is also noted for, however, is the writers and intellectuals who have lived there, studied there or who have written about it.

Mohamed Choukri, just for starters, the protegé of Paul Bowles and perhaps Morocco's most univerally respected writer, was educated there. His books included "For Bread Alone" and "The Lemon."

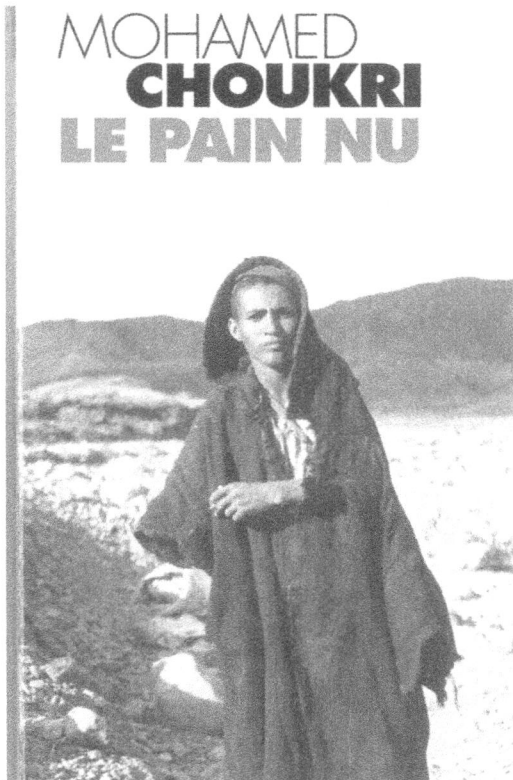

'For Bread Alone' with the author pictured on the cover

If there is just one book you would like to read about old Morocco from the point of view of the Moroccans, one could not recommend "For Bread Alone" highly enough. The title is a denial of the bibilical words "man shall not live by bread alone." The book was banned in Morocco but has sold 120,00 copies internationally.

In his book Choukri tells his life story, growing up in extreme poverty just after World War II in the Rif region and his family coming to Tangier to find bread. The descriptions of poverty and of his father's murdering cruelty are truly excruciating.

Choukri was illiterate but at the age of twenty started to teach himself reading and writing. Through the help of a friend he was able to get a place at a school in Larache where there was a sympathetic headmaster. So at the age of twenty one he became in his own words "the oldest and most depraved primary schoolboy in history."

It was through the help of this Larache headmaster, and later on of Paul Bowles, that Choukri developed into probably Morocco's leading writer.

Larache in the 1970s

Paul Okken begins:
I had become friendly in my country Holland with someone who later travelled out to Larache, with his wife, to be the manager of the Hotel de Espana. He afterwards invited me out to visit the town and have a holiday there, so it was really just by chance that I found it.

Hotel de Espana is situated right on the main square of the town. I say "square" but in fact the Plaza de Espana is a circular town centre, with about five streets converging there. It is set out in a traditional way with a fountain in the middle and cafés all the way round the edge of the ring. When I arrived I was amazed at how wild the place was – you could hardly reach a café without a group of young locals accosting you and offering friendship or wanting money.

The fountain usually had a group of the quieter and older ones sitting there, hoping that you would ignore the more brazen younger ones, whom they disapproved of. (I'm told they have now put an iron fence round it, I guess to stop the lads sitting around it.)

Spanish was the only language spoken apart from Arabic. There were single European men around, but not as many as in Tangier or Agadir. I had, however, never liked Tangier as I found many of the young Rif inhabitants there very rough and unpredictable. Not that they were always so smooth in Larache – but most of them were fine, and I always managed to find a very nice friend or two for the holiday.

I think the café called the Atlantic Balcony was a good place to socialise with other Europeans – usually middle-aged or older – and also with younger Moroccan ones who would be selling things. On the other hand the main meeting place for the local Moroccans was the Café Central on a corner of the Plaza de Espana.[37] .

I did occasionally take a young Moroccan into Larache's main cinema, where the back seats of the gallery were the most fun!

Larache's cinema in 1960s, with Hotel de Espana in the distance right

But even more fun than the cinema was the beach. I must explain that the town was situated on one side of the river but the beach was on the other, so in those days you had to get into one of the many small boats to take you across. Going across on a little boat was always entertaining, and I remember there was sometimes a band playing in one of the other boats to serenade us as we crossed!

---

[37] Café Central was also Mohamed Choukri's favourite meeting place during his years there.

*Swimming on the town side of the river by the rocks (above),
or on the other side of the estuary where there was a beach.*

Once you'd crossed the estuary and were over there, you would often have the beach more or less to yourselves and you could do whatever you wanted to with your friend. But if there were other people around you could go further on into the sand-dunes.

Another place I loved visiting in the town was the tapas bar called Estrella del Mar (Star of the Sea) where I enjoyed the rough, raunchy atmosphere and where you could easily get chatting and making friends with those lovely men. There was also a window in the upstairs bar which looked onto the sea port and you could watch the boats coming in and out too (whereas most Moroccan bars aren't allowed windows for fear people might see the shameful drinking habits of those inside).

I am told Jean Genet would sometimes drink in the Estrella del Mar, but I never saw him in there myself. However, I did once spot him sharing a bottle of wine with a group of down-and-outs right down on the rocks by the sea, way below the Atlantic Balcony – he loved mixing with the lowest in society.

Now Rowan Tudor continues:
I always enjoyed my trips to Larache in the 1960s and 1970s, although I found the older square behind more interesting for contact with locals than the Plaza de Espana itself. They would sit in a row along a wall there.

The old square in Larache was rather hidden away

Often the opening line would be "You know la Foret Diplomatique?" They assumed that anyone who knew it would be only interested in one thing!

Now Tim Vaughan:
I had gone on a holiday around 1990 to Larache with my friend Martin Croydon. We had a very pleasant time. We managed to find a

downstairs flat in the house of a European family; the children of whom could not have been more charming and Martin kept in touch with the family by letter for some time after. We also found two cousins who were shoe-shiners and who became our friends in a very relaxed and good-natured way.

I also remember the trips across the estuary to the beach. I always went across in one of the small boats – as it was good for my hay fever, although of course Martin told everyone it was just for me to get close to those muscular young men doing the rowing! On the way back, however, we would both catch the bus, which took quite a while in those days before they had built the new bridge, with the bus going right along one side of the estuary, crossing the old bridge and returning along the other side.

What always struck us during this bus ride was how well-behaved all the children and young people were, of absolutely every age from three months to thirty. It would have been grim in the UK.

On one occasion there was a baby who started crying and a lad of about fourteen in his swimming trunks offered to have the baby on his lap. The mother looked greatly relieved and grateful, watching while the lad (probably from a big family himself) very gently rocked the baby and stopped it crying. That just wouldn't happen in England, would it? – and more's the pity.

Back to Tony on authors in Larache:
I had better start by saying that most of these authors were not, as far as I know, specifically gay – in that respect different to most of those in Tangier perhaps. Some of the authors in Larache had been born there, gone to Spain to work, but then returned, calling themselves Larachenses (in much the same way as the expats in Tangier called themselves Tangerinos). They seemed to have returned almost as a pilgrimage, and it's surprising that there is no university there.

For example, "Voyages to Larache" is a book by Mohamed Laabi describing voyages through the ages made by Spanish travellers coming to the town by sea. He has also brought together the works of the town's several poets in another book "Voices of Larache."

To give just two more of the many Larache authors: firstly the best-known one, Sergio Barce Gallardo, lived there until his parents took him to Malaga. His most famous novels are "Latest News From Larache" and "Sombras en Sepia" – the latter winning a top literary prize, competing with writers from all over Spain. (You will notice how often the word "Larache" comes into the titles.)

Secondly, Mohamed Sibari sought to keep the Spanish culture alive in North Morocco through his books, including "From Larache to the Sky". Based on truth, this is about an Arab boy growing up in moderate poverty in Larache and Tangier. He is not helped by having a very fair skin and 'pretty boy' looks.

"From Larache to the Sky"

The young man is helped even less by his pressurised conversion to Catholicism, which makes him a traitor in some of the people's eyes. Eventually, however, through the intervention of Marshall Mohamed Amezian – who had himself deftly changed sides at the right moment – he is able to join the newly independent Moroccan airforce. So the poor lad had to prove his manhood twice over. (Which just shows that possessing a pretty face does have its drawbacks.)

It's time now to hear about Morocco's second most famous expat after Paul Bowles, namely Jean Genet – perhaps France's most influential gay writer since André Gide.

Genet (1910–1986) lived in Larache for the last eight years of his life. France's greatest gay novelist, poet and playwright, he wrote his final work "A Loving Captive" there. This was inspired by the Shatila massacre of Palestinians, for whom Genet had huge sympathy in their struggle against Israeli/American oppression.

Genet in a Palestinian refugee camp in 1971

Wherever he travelled in the Palestinian territories Genet had come face to face with, and written about, their suffering. He had himself been a soldier in the region. And his memories of all the times spent with Palestinians had been intensified for him by spending the night with a young fighter, Hamza, in his family home.

We can't fully understand the older Genet without knowing what happened to him as a young man. At the age of sixteen he had been convicted of theft and sent to reform school – beginning a life always in touch with minor criminals. He escaped at the age of nineteen, joining the Foreign Legion but deserting after a few days. Always a rebel, he lived by begging, narcotics and prostitution.

Crimes became for Genet "a ritual with religious overtones". He was caught and sent several times to prison, where he wrote poems, novels and plays. The Mettray prison colony, to the south west of Paris, was where he had his first gay love affair. He called it "a sexually charged Garden of Eden." (There was maybe something of a tradition in French literary circles, started by Rimbaud and Verlaine, of the poet often not only being gay/bisexual but also bohemian, disreputable and rebellious.)

Police mug shot of young Genet

In 1948 Genet was sentenced to life imprisonment as a habitual criminal. It was only through the statements by Jean Cocteau and Jean Paul Sartre that they considered him to be a genius, that he was given a reprieve.

Back to Genet's last years in Larache. In his old age the nearness of the port was probably some consolation to him. (As Kenneth Williams used to say: "We are all behind the Royal Navy!"). To give you an even more relevant quote from "Querelle," Genet's novel set in another port, Brest: "All those lithe and lusty lads licked into shape by and for a training in seamanship, with the stamp of their calling in their rolling gait, in the sturdy set of their shoulders and in their rollicking provocative buttocks."

The port of Larache, loved by Genet

Whilst living and writing in Larache he arranged for the construction of a house there for his final lover, Mohamed el Katrani, whom he had met in Tangier sleeping on the pavement.

During their relationship Katrani had a son by a woman from whom he became estranged. Genet himself named the boy Azzedine and became very attached to him, as well as to Katrani, virtually adopting the boy as his grandson. The house he had built for his adopted family was at the southern end of the Atlantic Balcony, with a large tree in its courtyard – and the nearby cemetery would become Genet's final resting-place. (Even though a large room was kept in the house for Genet, he preferred right to the end, typically, to stay in one of the most downmarket hotels by Larache's old square.)

In his final years of his life Genet desperately needed money to pay the fees for Azzedine's private education, and he agreed to be interviewed more than once for TV, although he hated having to explain his life in front of a camera. He also made a successful film named "Un Chant d'Amour," as well as both writing and directing a play set in the Algerian War called "The Screens." (Needless to say he was passionately against his country's involvement in that war.) One of his plays, "The Maids", was a commercial success.

Yet it is the novels that he will be mainly remembered for, novels which "shattered the barriers in the treatment of homosexuality in literature." At the same time, some of the greatest philosophers of the twentieth century, such as Sartre, Derrida and Foucault, held Genet in great esteem.

Photo taken at south end of Larache, near to the house built for Katrani & Azzedine, and close to where Genet is buried.

41
Tangier Epilogue
by Tony Walton

A chance introduction

The whole story of Tangier for me was something one read about as history and assumes it had now completely changed. I had imagined, for example, that all the famous literary people who had lived there would, by the time of the twenty-first century, have either passed away, like Paul Bowles for example, or have gone to live elsewhere.

But I then had a most unexpected piece of luck. Whilst telling a friendly acquaintance, David Aprahamian Liddle, about my future project of editing these memoirs, he surprised me by saying he could get me an introduction to one of the last remaining expatriate authors there, Patrick Thursfield. Patrick, in addition to being fairly well-known himself[38] would have met most of the Tangier literati, including Paul Bowles.

I was both very excited but also surprised, as David has never visited Morocco. The explanation was this: David has had an almost lifelong interest in the story of Peter Wildeblood, the famous homosexual pioneer campaigner of the 1950s, who for a while had lived in Tangier. David devoted a lot of time finding out about and recording the later life of this campaigner who was, in effect, a martyr to the cause of gay acceptance. So let's now hear from David:

"I endeavoured to make contact with those who had been close to (Wildeblood). A dear Canadian friend of mine said he had once met him, and he had friends who knew the nurse that had cared for him during his last illness. In due course, I telephoned the male nurse in Victoria Island BC, and had the first of many lovely, long conversations.

"The nurse could tell how fascinated I was with Peter's life, and how I tend to remember a great deal of what I am told. He promised to enquire with two close friends of Peter's whether they would be willing to talk to me. Later I became friendly with both: firstly Peter's partner of twenty years and his Oxford contemporary,

---

[38] There is a potted biography at end of this chapter, "The last of the Tangerinos"

and secondly the author Patrick Thursfield, residing in Tangier. The former I met, correspond and speak with regularly; the latter I never met but we have exchanged several letters and phone calls...

Peter Wildeblood

"Patrick's letters to me (from Tangier) about Peter Wildeblood are documentary treasures. In one he told how he drove Peter to his parents' home in Sussex to break the news of his arrest in connection with gay offences. Patrick's support for Peter at this time cost him his own job on the Telegraph – simply by association.

"Peter and Patrick both acquired houses in Tangier. Peter's was more of a holiday home, which he later sold when he moved to Canada. Patrick settled in Tangier where he enjoyed a thriving social life and was a celebrated host."

This then was the Tangier legend with whom David so kindly helped me to get in touch. When I plucked up courage to phone Patrick from London I found him polite and accessible, and he proceeded, following only a small hint from me, to invite me to meet him that summer if I were willing to visit him in Tangier.

Reaching Tangier on 11th July 2003, I stayed in the small and economical Hotel Muniria[39], perched high on a steep hill overlooking the port, with a magnificent view across to Spain.. So many famous people had stayed there that I felt a real frisson of excitement on being shown to my room, knowing that Burroughs, Kerouac, Truman Capote or Allen Ginsberg would probably have been in that room, or one next door, at some stage.

Also, in the garden flat of the Muniria, William Burroughs had written part of "The Naked Lunch" (He was said to have occasionally thrown his typewriter out of one of the upstairs rooms when he saw phalluses coming out and so he was moved downstairs into what is now the Tanger Inn.)

The Tanger Inn (left), in the garden of the Muniria

---

[39] You will have read Paul Horler's excellent account in Chapter 23

Living amongst the greats

So the following morning I phoned Patrick from the Muniria, and he responded favourably by inviting me to lunch that same day. Having given me his car's registration number he said he would send his chauffeur and car down to the Café Metropole (an elegant café with outside tables and a good place to watch the world), to take me back.

The Metropole, one of the elegant 1920s cafes on Boulevard Pasteur

I arrived at the café before the agreed time and drank a coffee, peering at each car to see if it had the right number. After about ten minutes, however, all the cars suddenly stopped, with a dreary silence descending on the street. The waiter whispered to me that all traffic had been sealed off – as the king was in town!

A frantic second phone call to Patrick confirmed that his chauffeur had tried to get through the blockade three times. He was very happy, however, to reschedule the visit to the afternoon with an invitation to have tea with him. I told him I could easily take a taxi, and so at 4.30, instructing the taxi driver to take me to La Vieille Montagne, number 189, I was at last on my way to meet the last of the Tangier literary legends.

Patrick's house sat pleasantly halfway up a hill in the area which had the slightly camp name of Sidi Miss Musi, officially Arrondisement Three, but always referred to in books as "The Mountain," probably an Arab mistranslation of "hill". Most of the literati of Tangier finished up buying or renting houses in this fashionable area, and I was reminded of Rupert Croft-Cooke's description of Tangier in the 1950s as an "oriental Cheltenham."

Patrick welcomed me in his dressing gown, true Noel Coward style, and asked his servant to bring us both tea and cakes. He said his health had not been good lately and he needed to have a very long rest in the afternoons. I told him how much I appreciated his going to all this trouble, and he put me at my ease.

His house was a mixture of elegance and slightly worn forlornness, although it was surprisingly cool in the hot weather of that day, with a conservatory straight in front of the living room filled right up with large overhanging plants, and providing shade for the whole room, which was filled with books. I could just spot a pleasant, slightly neglected garden, then a view across town and bay.

He said his main work as a writer had been to translate the works of the Hungarian Miklos Bannfy into English. He explained, pointing to a map on the wall, how badly Hungary had been treated after WWI, losing many of its Magyar speaking areas. Luckily he was impressed with my knowledge of the 1919 peace treaties, but I was even more impressed with him when he said he had mastered the Magyar language, as it's notoriously hard to learn.

Clearly now I had to ask him direct questions about famous Tangier people. David Herbert? Patrick always found him "the most terrible snob," although Herbert was very much in awe of Paul Bowles. Yes, Patrick had sometimes gone to the famous Herbert parties, which he enjoyed. Had he attended the fancy dress one where Barbara Hutton was dressed as Peter Pan and Herbert as a pantomime dame? Yes he had – and he felt their costumes should have been reversed. [40]

(I would recommend readers to get hold of Herbert's autobiography, "Second Son," which gives a humorous view of Tangier high society in the 1960s. Patrick was probably hurt that he wasn't mentioned in it – although at the same time one feels he might have been incandescent with rage if he *had* been.)

On asking him about the "Beat Generation" Patrick said he'd known none of them except Brion Gysin, and him only because he

---

[40] See the photo on page 92 and judge for yourself.

had run a well-known restaurant called 'The Thousand And One Nights,' which he'd visited [41]. William Burroughs, he said, was a complete reclusive and very few people in Tangier had ever met him, or the other characters at the Muniria, let alone got to know them – even some of the many now claiming to have done so.

Not much gained on that one, but I persevered......David Edge? Yes, Patrick had known the other David, rival socialite David Edge, whom he rather liked even though he was known to be completely bogus in his claimed aristocratic connections. Edge was, he said, wildly eccentric in a way that David Herbert only pretended to be. Edge kept a semi-savage boy in his house in the Kasbah as his personal servant, whom he had rescued from the backwoods of Spain and was trying to civilise, like the 'enfant sauvage' of Aveyron.

Patrick had met the boy? Yes, and he seemed to be completely in awe of his surroundings and bemused by what was happening. Patrick explained that Edge's house had formerly been a harem, square in shape with alcoves round a fountain and everything done up in black and gold. Everyone wanted to visit it having heard its reputation and sometimes fights would break out in the queue of people outside trying to get in!

But Patrick had visited it? Yes, several times.

Eager to keep him on the subject of Morocco and of his many years spent there, I asked him if he had written any books about his life and friends in Tangier .

He replied that he had indeed done so, and with a dramatic sweep handed me a copy of his book of short stories/observations entitled "The Tangier Cat House, and other stories."

A note to the reader like myself, slipped into the front of the signed copy, explained "I have called the collection 'Cautionary Tales for Idle Expatriates,' as in the process of living amongst the Dodos – and in the process of becoming one myself – I have had an unrivalled opportunity of observing the sort of antics with which my expatriate friends and neighbours have diverted themselves."

The book is indeed very entertaining in its portrayal of expat eccentrics and local gossip – in some ways, I suppose, like this one

---

[41] see Chapter 21, on famous bars.

tries to be. Of course his book gives little away on a certain more personal subject, and I was reminded of how Paul Bowles, Patrick's contemporary fellow writer in Tangier, after publishing his autobiography with the title "Without Stopping", had it called "Without Telling" by some of his friends.

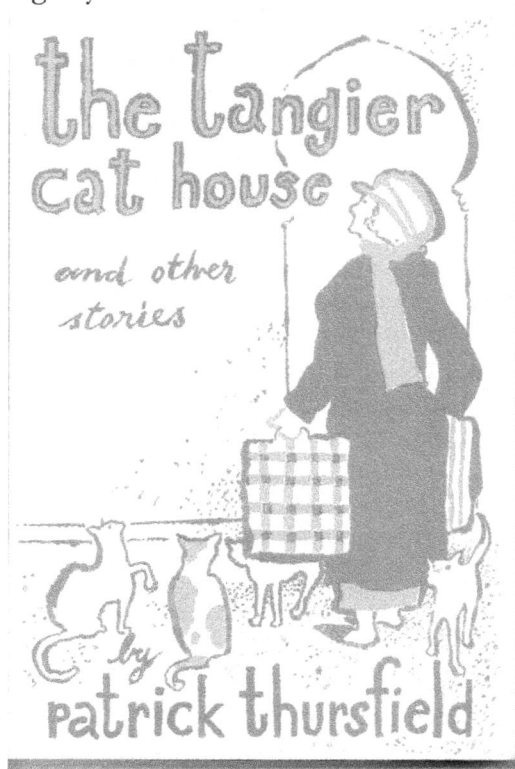

Returning to Rupert Croft-Cooke, Patrick paid tribute to the fact that he "came out" as gay, but he said David Herbert never quite forgave him for that. One has to remember that as gay men they were all living through dangerous and insecure times, with different people adopting different strategies to survive. For example Herbert had complained, when RCC arrived in Tangier, that they would all have "to put up with having a jailbird around." (I suppose they would have seen the international city of Tangier as a safe haven and wouldn't want anyone spoiling it by being too bold or notorious. David Aprahamiam Liddle's story in the first part of this chapter mentioned how Patrick had helped Peter Wildeblood at great cost to himself, and it's all too easy for us now to forget the pains and challenges of gay life then.)

Patrick then mentioned Michelle Green's book "The Dream at the End of the World", subtitled "Paul Bowles and the Literary Renegades of Tangier.". He said he had made contributions to it but only on the express understanding that his comments were not to be acknowledged in the book. This probably reflects on how touchy people could be in a small expatriate community and how much offence could be taken if they considered they were being written about with too little accuracy, or conversely with too much honesty.

That brought us nicely onto the subject of Paul Bowles. Patrick said he had always found Paul very reserved but his wife and fellow-writer Jane (whom he called 'Janey') very pleasant and charming. It occurred to me afterwards that she was the only person mentioned in the interview whom he seemed to have really liked – she had sadly died quite young in 1973 in Spain after a long and dreadful illness

Unexpectedly, Patrick then started talking about the Beat Generation again, mentioning how Bowles had become their "patron saint" after his book "A Hundred Camels in the Courtyard" was published in 1962. Hippies or druggies would arrive at his front door either to find out how to write the best book in the world, or just to meet the great man. People used to literally sit in queues outside but he never sent anyone away – and Patrick felt Janey found this hard to cope with.

An earlier book of Bowles turned into a film, "The Sheltering Sky", was a strange story about a husband and wife dropping out of Tangier society and wandering off into the desert. According to the blurb on the back it was the origin of the philosophy of "Cool", although I think the word has changed its meaning nowadays. I asked him if he knew the book. Yes he did, but he felt that the book was daring for its day but "would be considered tame now." He may have slightly under-estimated the disturbing quality which the book has, for me at least, even now.

I then asked Patrick about bars in the town of interest or notoriety in the past. He said he had found both The Parade and The Tanger Inn very dull, and he felt by far the best bar in the old days was the Bar Safari, not far from the Parade, which sometimes had a band playing. Patrick said he had never been in Dean's Bar – slightly surprising as it's near the centre of the town and you will have read its fascinating history in Chapter 21. He had naturally read "The Wrong People" (which starts off in Dean's Bar) and had found it very readable, although he felt the book had "got the active and passive round the wrong way." I asked him what he meant and he explained that Maugham suggested that European men had wanted to take the active sexual role with Moroccans in Tangier, whereas Patrick felt they much more often wanted the passive.

Had he met Barbara Hutton? Yes, and he had attended parties at her house, Sidi Hosni, where he had also met one of her later lovers, a young man named Lloyd Franklin. Patrick felt the latter was rather out of his depth and followed Barbara round like a puppy. The idea that all of her men-friends were just in it for the money was unfair, he said, and Lloyd really did seem devoted to her.

At the end of the long interview I expressed my very genuine thanks to him for his time, effort and for the copy of his book. I mentioned the fact that Paul Horler, our researcher, would probably like to meet him. He said he would be delighted to meet Paul.

This was sadly not to be as, only six weeks after the interview, I received the news from David that Patrick had passed away.

The last of the Tangerinos

Patrick Thursfield was born in 1923 not far from Nelson's birthplace in Norfolk. He attended Charterhouse School and Oxford.

He served in World War Two in the RNVR, combined operations, serving with the Marines in the Far East – as did also David Herbert, although they never met there.

Amongst his journalistic jobs after the war was that of diplomatic correspondent for the Times. However, when Peter Wildeblood was released from prison he went to the prison gate to meet him, and for this "offence" Patrick was dismissed from his job by the Western Press Group, a reminder of just how anti-homosexual the atmosphere was in the UK in the 1950s.

Later on he made three trips to visit Peter in Vancouver after the latter had had a stroke, and it was considered by others that these visits greatly helped Wildeblood to make a complete recovery.

Patrick's books included translations of the works of Miklos Banffy, the Hungarian writer, which he did in collaboration with

Banffy's daughter Katalin. The last one, called "They Were Divided", won a Weidenfeld Translation Prize.

Allan Ramsey, the British ambassador to Morocco in the 1990s, described Thursfield after his death as "the last of the Tangerinos", meaning probably the last of those mostly quite well off, and in varying degrees both literary and gay, expats who made Tangier their home during the middle part of the twentieth century.

Patrick lived next door to Malcolm Forbes, the multi-million American magazine proprietor (who was famous for his collection of toy soldiers, but also for the two million dollar birthday party he threw in 1989!). He also had a long but slightly difficult relationship with David Herbert and does not in fact seem to have had many close friendships with the other male Tangerinos.

Patrick was also out of sympathy with the movements for gay rights back in England, considering sexuality was not something you should shout about. He was perhaps always just a bit of an outsider looking in but, having said that, he was generally sociable amongst the Tangerinos and a good host. He also had platonic but warm friendships with Jane Bowles, as well as with a female member of the Moroccan royal family.

When Patrick sent a draft of "The Tangier Cat House" to his friend Francis King, the well-known novelist, the latter replied with this message: "I have often envied you living in such beautiful surroundings, but after reading your tales I realise there are serpents in your Paradise."

Maybe Francis King's words would make quite a good epitaph for old Tangier… and for some other North African cities too.

SELECTED BIBLIOGRAPHY

Bowles, Paul: *Without Stopping (New York 1972*

Bowles, Paul: *Two Years Beside the Strait (New York 1972)*

Burroughs WS & Gysin B: *The Third Mind (London 1990)*

Choukri, Mohamed: *For Bread Alone (London 1973)*

Croft-Cooke, Rupert: *The Caves of Hercules (London 1974)*

Davidson M: *The World, the Flesh and Myself (London 1962)*

Davies R: *Kenneth Williams Diaries*

Dillon M (ed): *Out in the World (Santa Barbara '85)*

Dynes, Wayne (ed):*Encylopaedia of Homosexuality
                (Chicago and London 1990)*

Edmonds Guide to Tangier(Tangier 1960)

Finlayson Iain: *Tangier, City of the Dream (London 1992)*

Fryer, John: *André and Oscar (London, 1999)*
Gide, André : *Strait is the Gate*

Gide, André : *If It Die*

Green, Michelle: *The Dream at the End of the World (London 1992)*

Herbert David: *Second Son (London 1972)*

Herve & Kerrest: *Les Enfants de Fez (Paris, 1980)*

Hopkins, John: *The Tangier Diaries 1962-1979 (london 1997)*

Lahr, John (ed): *The Orton Diaries (London 1986)*

Lahr, John: *Prick Up Your Ears (London 1978)*

Maugham, Robin: *The Wrong People (London 1970)*

Sawyer-Lauccano: *An Invisible Spectator (London 1989)*

Sibari, Mohamed: *De Larache al Cielo*

Stewart, Angus: *Tangier: a writer's notebook (London 1977)*

Vaidon L : *Tangier – a Different Way (NJ & London 1977)*

Woolman David: *Stars in the Firmament (Colorado 1998)*

Index